THE TERRORIST TRIAL OF THE 1993 BOMBING OF THE WORLD TRADE CENTER

A Headline Court Case

Headline Court Cases

THE TERRORIST TRIAL OF THE 1993 BOMBING OF THE WORLD TRADE CENTER

A Headline Court Case

Michael J. Pellowski

Enslow Publishers, Inc.

40 Industrial Road	PO Box 38
Box 398	Aldershot
Berkeley Heights, NJ 07922	Hants GU12 6BP
USA	UK

http://www.enslow.com

To my cousin Mickey Novack

Library of Congress Cataloging-in-Publication Data

Pellowski, Michael J.
   The terrorist trial of the 1993 bombing of the World Trade Center : a
headline court case / Michael J. Pellowski.
      p. cm. — (Headline court cases)
   Summary: Examines the trials of Mahmoud Abouhalima, Ramzi Yousef,
Mohammad Salameh, Sheik Omar Abdel-Rahman, and others for their roles in
the 1993 bombing of the World Trade Center.
   Includes bibliographical references and index.
   ISBN 0-7660-2045-2 (hardcover)
   1. Trials (Terrorism)—United States—New York (State)—New
York—Juvenile literature. 2. World Trade Center Bombing, New York,
N.Y., 1993—Juvenile literature. 3. Terrorism—New York (State)—New
York—Juvenile literature. [1. Trials (Terrorism) 2. Trials (Conspiracy)
3. World Trade Center Bombing, New York, N.Y., 1993. 4. Terrorism.]
I. Title. II. Series.
   KF224.W67 P45 2003
   974.7'1043—dc21
                              2002156033

Printed in the United States of America

10 9 8 7 6 5 4 3 2 1

To Our Readers: We have done our best to make sure that all Internet Addresses in this
book were active and appropriate when we went to press. However, the author and
publisher have no control over and assume no liability for the material available on those
Internet sites or on other Web sites they may link to. Any comments or suggestions can be
sent by e-mail to comments@enslow.com or to the address on the back cover.

Photo Credits: All photos are from AP/Wide World.

Cover Photo: AP/Wide World.

Contents

chapter one

SMOKE, TERROR, AND DEATH

GROUND ZERO, NYC— September 11, 2001, is an infamous date painfully scorched into the memories of most Americans. It is the day the Twin Towers of the World Trade Center (WTC) in New York City were attacked without warning and destroyed. On that day of national sorrow, terrorists finally succeeded in carrying out a diabolical plan first attempted some eight years earlier.

On February 26, 1993, a powerful bomb secreted in the basement parking area of the World Trade Center exploded. The force of the blast produced a scarred crater one hundred and fifty feet in diameter and five stories deep.

Sparks from the deadly explosion ignited pockets of fire and sent funnels of thick, gray smoke billowing toward the sky. Within ten minutes of the explosion, smoke had reached the forty-third floor. It filled the hallways and offices, choking and blinding the occupants of the building. Thousands of innocent civilians were injured in the blast, and six people lost their lives.

The 110-story World Trade Center was rocked by the explosion, but it did not come crashing down as planned by the extremists who masterminded and executed the attack. The 1993 plot to topple the towers failed. However, the terrorists did succeed in another way. For the first time in modern history, the homeland security of the United States was threatened by an expertly trained and well-organized worldwide terrorist network. U.S. citizens finally realized that America was not safe from attack.

A Day of Terror

"Next time it will be very precise," noted terrorist Nidal Ayyad on his computer, which was recovered by government agents investigating the 1993 World Trade Center bombing.[1] Ayyad's prophecy was a terrible harbinger of future attacks.

"Terrorists have not only long memories, they have infinite patience," stated Edith E. Flynn, professor of criminal justice at Northeastern University, addressing the press on the increasing sophistication of modern terrorism. "They certainly learn from their mistakes."[2]

Terrorists did learn from the failure to bring down the World Trade Center towers in 1993. They learned that a bomb, no matter how powerful, was not the weapon necessary to destroy one of the world's sturdiest man-made wonders. A new and more effective weapon was selected to do the job. It was a weapon few experts believed could be

Emergency vehicles blocked the street near the World Trade Center following the bombing on February 26, 1993.

used for such a deadly purpose. In fact, it was not really a traditional weapon at all. It was a commercial jetliner.

On September 11, 2001—eight years after the 1993 attempt to destroy the World Trade Center—the most devastating terrorist onslaught ever waged against the United States occurred in the skies over Washington, D.C., Pennsylvania, and New York City. Militant fundamentalist Muslims seized four U.S. commercial airliners shortly after takeoff from airports on the East Coast.

The planes were filled with highly explosive jet fuel in anticipation of long coast-to-coast flights. Hijackers trained

FACTS ABOUT THE WTC COMPLEX

- Ground was broken for the World Trade Center in 1966, and the complex was dedicated in 1973.

- The World Trade Center was designed by architects Emery Roth and Minoru Yamasaki and the structural engineering firm of Skilling, Helle, Christiansen and Robertson.

- The World Trade Center was 110 stories and 1,350 feet high (the world's second tallest building after the Sears Tower in Chicago).

- The Towers were built using a braced tubular cantilever system with each wall being a rigid truss. Four trusses were joined at the corners, resulting in a continuous tube of square sections that resisted wind.

- The World Trade Center had its own underground mall.

- Some 130,000 people worked at or visited the World Trade Center each workday.

- The subway stations below the World Trade Center served over 100,000 riders each day.

as pilots stormed the cockpits and took over the controls. The jumbo jets altered their original courses. Two planes headed for Washington, D.C. Two others reversed direction and headed back toward the East Coast.

Later, one plane crashed into the Pentagon in Washington, D.C. Another Washington-bound plane was the scene of a courageous in-flight rebellion by passengers. That jet was prevented from reaching its destination and eventually crashed in a deserted Pennsylvania field.

The targets of the other jets were the World Trade Center towers in New York. At 8:48 A.M., the first hijacked Boeing 767 crashed into the north tower of the World Trade Center. Minutes later, the second jet smashed into the south tower.

Jet fuel spilled out, and massive fires ignited in both towers. A short time later, the south tower of the World Trade Center fell, crumbling and crashing to the earth. Within an hour, the north tower collapsed as well. Thousands of people from many nations died in the suicide attack. The entire civilized world was shocked and stunned by the event.

The words left behind by terrorist bomber Nidal Ayyad after the first attempt to destroy the World Trade Center in 1993 had come true. The World Trade Center had been destroyed by militant Muslim terrorists. The safety and serenity of American society had been challenged by an intricate network of suicidal fanatics.

America was quick to respond to the threat. A warning was issued to those responsible, saying that terrorism would be stamped out and people who supported terrorist activities would be hunted down and brought to justice.

"This battle will take time and resolve, but make no mistake about it, we will win," President George W. Bush vowed to the American people and to the world.[3]

Just as the hunt for terrorists continues today, the hunt for the conspirators involved in the 1993 WTC bombing began almost immediately. It was a long and difficult investigation. It ended in sensational, high-profile court cases. The baffling questions you have to decide for yourself are, Was justice truly served? Was the real truth uncovered?

Six people died and thousands were injured in the 1993 blast that rocked the World Trade Center. These three people use oxygen masks to help them breathe after their escape from the towers.

Did the final decisions in U.S. courts act as a deterrent or provocation to future terrorist acts?

One of the most puzzling and thought-provoking questions of all is, Were the two brutal acts of terrorism, one committed in 1993 and the other in 2001, somehow connected, and if so, in what ways? In the case of the 1993 World Trade Center bombing, the evidence of the prosecution and the defense will allow you to judge for yourself.

chapter two

A PLOT UNRAVELS

THE TWIN TOWERS—The world's second largest building and the workplace of more than 50,000 people shook and trembled when a massive explosion in the parking basement below the World Trade Center detonated at 12:18 P.M. on Friday, February 26, 1993. Hundreds of alarmed workers poured out of the smoke-filled towers into the streets of lower Manhattan. Their faces were black with soot. Their eyes were wide in fear. They gasped for air as they stumbled to safety.

Inside the buildings, others were trapped in elevators frozen by the blast. Some workers, who stayed in their offices to await help, smashed windows to allow fresh air to flow in and smoke to escape. On the ninety-fourth floor, eight disabled people waited to be rescued because they were unable to reach the street. High above on the observation deck, some two hundred terrified elementary school children were stranded.

Far below the towers,

the noon explosion brought down the steel and concrete ceiling of the underground Port Authority Trans Hudson (PATH) train station, a major transportation point for commuters. A fleet of U.S. Secret Service cars was also damaged by the blast.

People in surrounding buildings felt the force of the explosion. "It felt like an earthquake," said Mary Romano, a worker across the street in the World Financial Center.[1]

"There were vibrations for about fifteen seconds," stated Ron Schwartz, who also worked at the World Financial Center.[2]

Police and fire rescue teams rushed to the site to help. Many people walked down to safety through dark, smoky stairwells. Eventually, the children trapped on the observation deck were escorted to street level by police. Eight disabled people were taken to the roof and evacuated by helicopters. In all, twenty-three people, including a pregnant woman, were rescued from the towers by helicopter.

At first, the cause of the explosion was in question. Officials did not know if the blast was an accidental malfunction or the result of a bomb. James Fox, an assistant director of the Federal Bureau of Investigation (FBI) who headed the Bureau's New York office, initially told reporters that no bomb fragments had been found at the site.

Jack Killorin, a spokesman for the Bureau of Alcohol, Tobacco and Firearms (ATF) said a bombing could not be ruled out, but neither could an accidental blast.

It was New York Governor Mario Cuomo who bluntly stated exactly what most people already suspected. "It looks

HEIGHTS OF FAMOUS SKYSCRAPERS

Sears Tower (Chicago)—1,450 feet

World Trade Center (New York)—1,350 feet

Empire State Building (New York)—1,250 feet

Standard Oil Building (Chicago)—1,136 feet

John Hancock Building (Chicago)—1,127 feet

Chrysler Building (New York)—1,046 feet

Eiffel Tower (Paris, France)—986 feet

like a bomb. It smells like a bomb. It probably is a bomb."[3] When the governor later did an interview on the television show *Larry King Live*, Cuomo revealed the exact cause of the explosion. "It has been established that it was a bomb placed on the floor of the parking garage," he said.[4]

New York City Police Commissioner Raymond Kelly supported the governor's comments based on traces of nitrate found at the scene combined with the amount of heat and damage caused by the blast. The evidence definitely pointed to an act of terrorism rather than an accident.

The total number of people injured in the bombing was 1,042. Of those, four hundred required hospitalization. Sadly, six people lost their lives in the bombing:

- William Macko, a forty-seven-year-old New Jersey man

- Stephen Knapp, a forty-eight-year-old man from New York

- Robert Kirkpatrick, a sixty-one-year-old man from New York

- John DiGiovanni, a forty-five-year-old resident of New York

- Wilfredo Mercado, a thirty-seven-year-old New York–area man

- Monica Rodriguez Smith, a thirty-five-year-old New York woman who was pregnant when she died

The deaths were tragic, yet under the circumstances, the toll was lower than it could have been.

"I just marvel that more people weren't killed given the location and the hour," New York mayor David Dinkins told reporters two days after the incident.[5]

The Explosive Device

Special agents from the FBI Explosives Unit confirmed that the damage at the World Trade Center site had been caused by a homemade explosive device.

After an initial inspection of damage done to automobiles, concrete, and structural steel in the underground parking area, the examiners determined that the explosion was a pushing and heaving type of blast. Commercial explosives (dynamite or fertilizer-based explosives) produce an explosion of that type, while TNT and C–4 cause shattering and splitting. It was also determined that the main charge must have been between twelve hundred and fifteen hundred pounds. Based on this, the experts judged that the bomb had been too large to transport in a sedan type of

At first, the cause of the blast at the WTC was unknown, but officials soon revealed that it was a bomb. Above, New York City Police Commissioner Raymond Kelly speaks with reporters two days after the explosion.

automobile. The ceiling clearance of the entrance to the basement parking garage also limited the height of any large type of truck. The investigators were well on their way to finding out that the bomb had been transported to the World Trade Center parking area in either a pickup truck or a van.

Investigators realized that the carnage at the World Trade Center was the result of a terrorist bombing. They knew that the bomb had been driven into the parking basement in a van or a pickup truck. The main question still remained unanswered: Who was responsible for the horrible act that had left six people dead and over a thousand injured?

Shortly after the blast, ATF spokesman Jack Killorin announced that the authorities had received at least nine telephone calls from various radical groups claiming responsibility for the act. However, there was no evidence linking any known terrorist group to the bombing. (Terrorist groups seek publicity of any kind to bring their causes before the public eye, even if it means taking credit for newsworthy events they had no actual part in.)

New York governor Mario Cuomo pointed out that the attackers were attempting to instill fear and disrupt the everyday routine of American life. On February 27, 1993, he told reporters:

> Fear is another weapon that's used against you. And that's what terrorists are all about, if these were terrorists. And what they're trying to do is deny you normalcy and what we must do in this safest and greatest city and state and nation in the world is return as quickly as we can to normalcy.[6]

Governor Jim Florio of New Jersey, New York's neighbor across the Hudson River, expressed concern about the possibility of terrorist acts on America's home shores. Two days after the bombing, he said:

> This is a new problem. . . . If we are entering into a new chapter in American society, one that we've been free from in the past . . . we're going to have to start thinking about things like access to weapons and explosives and guns with a more focused attention.[7]

On Sunday, February 28, 1993, forensic chemists from the ATF, the FBI, and the New York Police Department (NYPD) were combing the wreckage in the World Trade Center basement. Donald Sadowy, a detective in the NYPD bomb squad, and Joe Hanlin, an ATF explosives expert, found a fragment from a vehicle frame that had massive explosive damage. The two investigators quickly recognized the fragment as an important lead.

One day earlier, Malcolm Brady, the supervisor of the ATF's national response team in the Northwest, had made a bold statement to reporters concerning clues that might lead to the apprehension of the bombers. "Find the vehicle," Brady said, "and you'll find the suspects."[8]

Sadowy and Hanlin had discovered a piece of what was believed to be the vehicle used to transport the bomb. The fragment was taken to a laboratory for closer inspection. Investigators then realized the twisted and scarred pieces of metal displayed a dot matrix number. The number was a vehicle identification number, which could be used to trace the owner of the vehicle believed to have contained the explosive device. The number identified the vehicle as a 1990 Ford F–350 Econoline van owned by Ryder Rental Agency, a large nationwide fleet of rental vehicles. That particular vehicle had been rented from a small local company, DIB Leasing, located across the river in Jersey City, New Jersey.

Agents of the FBI traveled to New Jersey to interview the office manager of DIB Leasing. The agents learned the van had been reported stolen. While the interview was in progress, a man named Mohammad Salameh telephoned the rental company to ask for his security deposit back. Salameh wanted the money returned because, he claimed, the 1990

Police survey the damage done by the bomb placed in the underground parking garage of the World Trade Center. Investigators discovered that the bomb had been brought to the garage in a Ford Econoline van.

Ford F–350 Econoline van he had leased had been stolen. Salameh said that he had gone to the local police to report the theft the night before the World Trade Center bombing. He claimed the police refused to accept his report because he did not know the license plate number of the stolen van. The day of the explosion, Mohammad Salameh had reported the reputed theft to the leasing agency and finally obtained the vehicle's license plate number. He then filed a report with the police. Mohammad Salameh seemed to be the innocent victim of strange circumstances . . . but was he really?

Who Is Mohammad Salameh?

Mohammad Salameh is a Palestinian who entered the United States on a Jordanian passport. At the University of Jordan he had studied *sharia*, or Islamic law. At the time of the WTC bombing, Salameh was a twenty-six-year-old Muslim with a reputation for being a decent, mild-mannered young man. He had no official criminal record.

However, Mohammad Salameh was not unknown to local police and the FBI. He was one of many Arabs who had previously spent months outside a U.S. court peacefully protesting the trial of El Sayyid Nosair. Nosair was a cousin of Ibrahim El-Gabrowny. El-Gabrowny was Mohammad Salameh's cousin. El Sayyid Nosair was accused of murdering an American Jewish militant named Meir Kahane.

Meir Kahane, an anti-Arab rabbi, was assassinated in New York in 1990. Nosair was eventually acquitted of the

Mohammad Salameh, shown here in a 1998 photo, telephoned the agency responsible for renting the vehicle that carried the bomb. He said the van had been stolen and asked to get his deposit back.

murder. However, he was jailed on weapons and assault charges.

El Sayyid Nosair was known to be a devoted disciple of Sheik Omar Abdel-Rahman, an Islamic religious leader who had been blinded by diabetes at age ten. Abdel-Rahman was a graduate of Al-Azhar, the Islamic world's most prestigious university, and he had many followers in Afghanistan. The sheik was strongly opposed to America's Mideast policies and supported armed opposition to the Israeli government.

The sheik was more than just an Egyptian scholar with radical views. Abdel-Rahman had been tried (and acquitted) in Egypt in connection with the assassination of Egyptian President Anwar Sadat.

In the minds of high-ranking FBI officials, Mohammad Salameh's association with Sheik Omar Abdel-Rahman, no matter how insignificant, made him a person to be watched.

Mohammad Salameh moved in militant circles well known to the FBI. The young Palestinian's connection to the van used in the bombing of the World Trade Center seemed more than just an innocent coincidence to FBI Agent William Atkinson. Was there a possible connection between Mohammad Salameh and the bombing? Was Sheik Omar Abdel-Rahman connected to the incident? Were radical Muslims involved in the terrorist act, and was the act a means of protesting America's involvement in the Middle East conflict? There were many puzzling questions to be answered by further investigation.

A Letter from Terrorists

On March 3, 1993, four days after the WTC bombing, *The New York Times* received a letter that claimed responsibility for the act. The letter was composed on a personal computer and printed on a laser printer. It read:

> We, the Fifth Battalion of the Liberation Army, declare responsibility for the explosion on the mentioned building. The action was done in response for the American political, economical and military support to Israel, the state of terrorism and the rest of the dictator countries in the region.
>
> Our demands are:
> Stop all military, economical and political aid to Israel.
> All diplomatic relations with Israel must stop.
> Not to interfere with any of the Middle East countries interior affairs.
>
> If our demands are not met, all of our functional groups in the Army will continue to execute our missions against military and civilian targets in and out of the United States. This will also include some potential nuclear targets, for your own information our army has more than hundred and fifty suicidal soldiers ready to go ahead. The terrorism that Israel practices (which is supported by America) must be faced with a similar one. The dictatorship and terrorism (also supported by America) that some countries are practicing against their own people must also be faced with terrorism.[9]

chapter three

ISLAM AND TERRORISM: A HISTORY

HISTORY—Terrorism is the actual or threatened use of violence for political purposes. It is directed not only against the targeted victims, but also against related groups and innocent people as well. It is a deadly and merciless form of undeclared warfare that thrives on notoriety.

International terrorism usually surfaces during times of political and social unrest. In the 1800s, terrorism was used by radical groups in Spain, France, and Italy. Terrorism played an important role in the Russian Revolution of 1917.

In the twentieth century, organizations such as the Croatian Ustashi, the Basque Separatist group ETA, and the Irish Republican Army used terrorism inside and outside their own countries in attempts to pursue various political goals and social demands.

In the 1960s, a broader form of more violent international terrorism appeared to threaten world peace and security. Technological advances made terrorism easier and more deadly. Weapons became smaller but more destructive. Rapid communication made connections between distant members of terrorist groups easy. International travel was also easier.

The form of terrorism that threatens world peace today originated with conflicts in the Middle East. Before the creation of the modern state of Israel in 1948, Jewish radical groups such as Irgun Zvai Leumi resorted to terrorism in their struggle with Arab and British adversaries. The expulsion of Palestinian guerrillas from Jordan in September 1970 resulted in the creation of the Arab terrorist group known as Black September.

The use of terrorist tactics rapidly spread beyond the Middle East after the 1960s. The Red Army Faction, sometimes called the Baader-Meinhof Gang, operated in West Germany. In 1977 the Red Army Faction kidnapped and murdered industrialist Hans-Martin Schleyer. Members of the same group also raided U.S. military installations abroad, robbed banks, and hijacked airliners.

An Italian terrorist group known as the Red Brigades kidnapped and murdered former Italian Prime Minister Aldo Moro in 1978. In 1980, terrorists in Italy bombed the Bologna railroad station.

Terrorist organizations also operate in Japan, the United States, and many other countries. Radical groups like Aum Shinrikyo in Japan have often targeted citizens of their own nation in their terrorist attacks. In the United States, organizations such as the Ku Klux Klan have harassed and murdered members of other racial, ethnic, and religious groups.

Some foreign governments have been identified as supporting various terrorist organizations. Libya, Southern Yemen, Algeria, and Afghanistan are among those countries known to have openly supported terrorist groups like the Palestine Liberation Organization (PLO) and Al Qaeda, the terrorist group headed by Osama bin Laden.

A Short History of the Middle East Conflict

The rivalry between Judaism and Islam has been a contributing factor in the Middle East conflict since ancient times. While Islam was established by the prophet Mohammed around 600 A.D., both Jews and Muslims trace the founding of their faiths to the prophet Abraham some four thousand years ago. According to religious tradition, Abraham's wife, Sarah, bore her husband a son when she was ninety years old. That son was Isaac. Because Abraham and Sarah went so many years without having a child, Abraham had a son with another woman before Isaac's birth. The woman was Hagar, Sarah's servant. The son Abraham had with Hagar was named Ishmael.

Both Ishmael and Isaac are considered to be important ancestors: Ishmael of the Arab tribes, Isaac of the Jewish people. Ishmael is an important figure in Islam. Isaac is an important figure in Judaism.

Conflict Over the State of Israel

The country that is called Israel by Jews and Palestine by Muslims is a prime part of the dispute between the two groups. Both Jewish and Muslim traditions hold that

Abraham was told by God to leave Mesopotamia and settle in the area that is now Israel. The Jews lived in Israel during biblical times, but the country fell to a series of invaders and the Jewish people were dispersed all over the world. The modern state of Israel was established in 1948 by the United Nations on what had been Arab land. Disputes over that land, the city of Jerusalem, and the religious rivalry between Muslims and Jews has spawned various armed conflicts and many terrorist acts.

Zionism was a movement to establish a Jewish state in Palestine, the ancient homeland of the Jews. It grew in response to the persecution of Jews in Europe during the nineteenth century. In 1897, Theodor Herzl presided over the first Zionist Congress in Basel, Switzerland.

In 1917 Great Britain was given a mandate, or order to rule, over Palestine. The British foreign secretary, Arthur Balfour, promised the Jewish people that he would help them secure an independent national home.

The number of Jews living in Palestine grew and grew, which troubled some Arab neighbors. In the late 1930s, Palestine's population was more than one-third Jewish. Some Arabs welcomed the Jews and sold them land. Others felt threatened. Savage conflicts erupted. There were violent acts of terrorism on both sides.

During World War II, the Nazis, under Adolf Hitler, killed 11 million civilians, including 6 million Jews—two thirds of the Jews in Europe. Jews from Europe who survived the mass murder, which came to be known as the Holocaust, fled to Palestine in large numbers. Great Britain and America supported making Israel a Jewish state. In 1948 the United Nations agreed to the partition (division) of Palestine and the creation of an independent state of Israel. War between Israel and the Arab states opposed to its creation began in 1948 and lasted until early 1949. Israel could not be defeated, but some Arab groups refused to end the ongoing battle. Most Arab states never officially recognized the new state of Israel.

The Dispute Over Jerusalem

Another key part of the Arab-Israeli conflict is the city of Jerusalem. Jerusalem is a sacred site to both Muslims and Jews. The prophet Mohammed is said to have led a congregational prayer of the prophets in the Al Aqsa Mosque in Jerusalem. Jerusalem is also revered by followers of the Jewish and Christian faiths. Control of the Holy City has been a matter of bloody conflict since the Crusades.

Beginning in 1948, Jerusalem was a divided city. West Jerusalem was held by Israel, and Jordan controlled East Jerusalem. In 1967 there was a border conflict between Israel and Egypt. After several skirmishes, Israel launched an attack on Egypt. Syria, Jordan, and Iraq, Egypt's allies, in turn attacked Israel. Israel destroyed the air forces of all four Arab states and defeated their ground troops as well, thus preventing an Arab invasion of Israel. Israeli troops captured more disputed land. In six days, the war was over, with Israel victorious. One important aspect of the conflict was that the city of Jerusalem was incorporated into the state of

An Israeli police officer stands guard in front of the Dome of the Rock, near Al Aqsa mosque in Jerusalem. This holy site, sacred to both Jews and Muslims, is a topic of contention between the two groups, like the city itself.

Israel. Jerusalem is now under Jewish control (although the city is open to followers of all faiths).

Terrorism in the Middle East

In the 1970s, terrorism with roots in the Mideast conflict was a common occurrence. One of the worst acts of terrorism took place at the 1972 Olympic Games in Munich, West Germany. Eight members of a Palestinian terrorist organization known as Black September stormed the Israeli compound at the Olympics. They killed one athlete and took nine others hostage. The terrorists demanded that two hundred Palestinians held in Israeli prisons be freed. When the Israeli government refused to negotiate, West German officials tried to lure the terrorists into a trap by promising them safe passage to Cairo, Egypt. A shoot-out followed. All nine hostages, five terrorists, and a German policeman were killed. The plot of the terrorists failed, but those who supported terrorism were pleased by the worldwide publicity the incident received.

In 1974 the plight of oppressed Palestinians living in Israeli-occupied territory became a worldwide concern. A man named Yasir Arafat addressed the United Nations about the issue. Arafat was the leader and founder of an Arab guerrilla movement known as the Palestine Liberation Organization. Israel refused to recognize Palestine as an independent Arab state.

President Anwar Sadat of Egypt was the first Arab head of state to officially recognize Israel's sovereignty. In 1978 President Sadat met with Israeli Prime Minister Menachem

Begin and U.S. president Jimmy Carter. Sadat and Begin signed a historic peace treaty. It was the first peace accord of any kind between Israel and an Arab state. The treaty was loudly denounced by the Palestine Liberation Army and other militant groups. Some Arabs even labeled President Sadat a traitor to Islam. Sadat was assassinated by Egyptian religious extremists in 1981.

The Revolution in Iran and the Rise of Fundamentalist Islam

Iran was the scene of a violent revolt in 1979. The Shah of Iran was opposed by Muslims who disliked the Shah's liberal attitude toward modern concepts and values. The Shah's dependence upon the United States was also a sore point that angered many Muslims. Opposition to the Shah was spearheaded by an Islamic religious leader, the Ayatollah Khomeini. Khomeini, who was in exile in France, called upon the army of Iran to overthrow the Shah and to establish an Islamic republic in Iran. The army heeded Khomeini's words, and the Shah was overthrown. Ayatollah Khomeini returned to Iran and took control of the Islamic republic he helped create.

Another new ruler rose to power in the Middle East in the late 1970s. His name was Saddam Hussein. Saddam Hussein took control of Iraq in 1979. Almost immediately, Iran's Ayatollah Khomeini called for a Muslim overthrow of Saddam's rule in Iraq. Even though the majority of Iraqis are Muslim, Saddam Hussein headed a nonsectarian political party (one that has no connection to any religious group).

Khomeini disliked Saddam's modern views and called his rule godless. Religion was a key issue of the conflict between Iraq and Iran.

Iraq then invaded Iran. Saddam hoped to gain control of a waterway at the head of the Persian Gulf that formed a border between the two countries. Iran had the support of Syria in the conflict. Iraq had the support of most Arab states and the West. During the conflict, Iraq used chemical weapons and was later condemned by the United Nations for doing so. In 1988, after many casualties on both sides, Iraq and Iran agreed to a cease-fire.

Lebanon became a Middle East hot spot in 1982. Half of Lebanon's people are Christian. The other half are Muslim. Lebanon was also the headquarters of the Palestine Liberation Organization. The mixed populace and the presence of Palestinians—especially members of the PLO—created a volatile atmosphere.

After an Israeli ambassador was shot by PLO terrorists in London, the state of Israel decided to retaliate. Twenty thousand Israeli soldiers invaded Lebanon and marched to the Lebanese capital of Beirut. Israeli troops beseiged Beirut for two months. The city was under savage bombardments. Yasir Arafat, the PLO leader, and his followers finally agreed to leave Lebanon if the siege was lifted. The Israeli bombardment left thousands of people dead and tens of thousands homeless. Most of the victims were Palestinians and Muslims. Many of the weapons used by Israel in the occupation of Lebanon were provided by the United States.

The 1980s and 1990s also saw the rise of a number of

fundamentalist Muslim governments in such countries as Sudan, Yemen, and Afghanistan. These governments attempted to enforce what they saw as the will of Allah by establishing strict Islamic laws. In some places, men were required to wear beards and women had to cover themselves completely in public. In some countries, women were also forbidden to hold jobs, drive cars, or go to school. Some of those who broke the law met with harsh punishments, even death.

War in the Persian Gulf

In the summer of 1990, Saddam Hussein upset the balance of power in the Middle East once again. The army of Iraq invaded neighboring Kuwait. The invasion resulted in the Gulf War of 1990. American forces, backed by Great Britain and twenty-seven other countries, stormed into the Middle East. After some short engagements with enemy forces, President Saddam Hussein agreed to a cease-fire. One result of the war was that Iraq agreed to limit its production of chemical weapons and weapons of mass destruction. Saddam agreed to allow United Nations inspectors into Iraq to inspect Iraq's weapons on a periodic basis. However, the inspectors were ousted from the country, leading to increased tensions between Iraq and the United States.

In 2002, President George W. Bush labeled Saddam Hussein a possible threat to America and the peace of the civilized world and asked for a United Nations declaration against Iraq. Weapons inspectors were readmitted to the country in late 2002.

In 2003, Saddam Hussein's refusal to disclose and dispose of weapons of mass destruction he was presumed to possess resulted in military action against his regime. A coalition force led by U.S. and British military units forcibly ousted Saddam's government in hopes of ensuring peace and reducing terrorist threats around the world.

The conflicts in the Middle East continue to play key roles in global affairs, especially since this area is the prime producer of the world's oil supply.

The Religion of Islam

The people involved in the 1993 and 2001 attacks on the World Trade Center are avowed followers of Islam. Members of Muslim terrorist groups often twist and bend the teachings of one of the world's great religions in an attempt to excuse their acts of violence and hate. Islam is not a religion that encourages violence or advocates hatred.

Islamic extremists who advocate the use of terrorism believe that the state of Israel and Judaism are serious threats to Islamic teachings. They also feel that their faith is threatened by Western culture and modern decadence. Radical Muslims have concerns about the effect of modern trends on young Muslims. They do not want followers of Islam to be corrupted by the temptations of modern civilization, which they feel are immoral.

Another reason radical Muslims give for their hatred of the United States is the presence of American troops in Saudi Arabia, site of the holy city of Mecca. (Saudi Arabia was a U.S. ally during the Gulf War.)

Islamic fundamentalists are resistant to change and progress and have little or no tolerance for people or nations that hold views that differ from their own. However, that is not the case among the vast majority of Muslims.

Islam was founded by the prophet Mohammed in what is now Saudi Arabia around 600 A.D. Islam endorses and encourages acts of peace and generosity as religious rules. The word "Islam" itself means "surrender or submission to the will of Allah." ("Allah" is Arabic for God.) In the eyes of Allah, all men are equal and brothers.

Followers of Islam revere Mohammed as the greatest prophet who ever lived and as the last messenger sent by God. Mohammed is honored, but so are many other prophets who preceded him, including Noah, Abraham, Moses, Ishmael, and Jesus, who is considered human rather than divine. In Islam, Allah rules alone.

Muslims believe that it was the task of the prophet Mohammed to bring to the world the revelation of Allah through the holy book of Islam, the Koran. In Mohammed's preaching, the prophet proclaimed not a new god but an all-powerful god of creation and judgment.

The followers of Islam are bound by certain duties listed in the Koran, known as the five pillars.[1] The first pillar is confession of faith. Followers declare the acceptance of God as the only god and of Mohammed as his prophet. Second comes prayer. At dawn, noon, late afternoon, sunset, and after nightfall, followers face the holy city of Mecca in *Salah* (ritual prayer).

Mecca is a city in Saudi Arabia, near the western coast

Devout Muslims pray five times daily. These boys are praying in the Abu-Hanifa mosque in Baghdad, Iraq.

of the Arabian peninsula; it is the birthplace of Mohammed. It is about forty miles inland from Jidda, a seaport on the Red Sea. Even before the time of Mohammed, Mecca was both a religious and a commercial center. In Mecca is a large mosque. In the center of the mosque is the Kaaba, a small temple of unknown age. In a wall of the Kaaba is the sacred Black Stone of Mecca, said to have been placed there by the prophet Abraham. Nearby is the sacred Zamzan Well associated with the story of Hagar and Ishmael in the Bible.

The third pillar of Islam is almsgiving. Followers of Islam are expected to be generous to those in need. People are required to give 2½ percent of their wealth; additional giving is encouraged. Charity is believed to purify a person's remaining wealth.

Fasting is also a pillar. During Ramadan, the holiest Islamic month, every healthy adult Muslim fasts from dawn to sunset, neither eating nor drinking. (Exceptions are made for nursing women, travelers, and soldiers on the march, though they are expected to fast later.) The purpose of fasting is to become pious and free from bad habits.

The last pillar is pilgrimage. All Muslims are required to make at least one pilgrimage to the city of Mecca during their lives. The pilgrimage is meant to encourage brotherhood and the exchange of ideas.

Key elements of Islam are concepts of brotherhood, sharing one's wealth, prayer, devotion, loyalty, and self-discipline. Those elements do not seem to support the claims of terrorists who insist their religion is the motive behind their violent actions.

chapter four

TRACKING THE TERRORISTS

WASHINGTON, D.C.— "The message we wish to send is that there is no ocean too wide, no distance too far, no time period too long and no effort too great to make those who kill or injure Americans immune from the U.S. justice system," said Attorney General Janet Reno when asked about the 1993 WTC bombing case.[1]

The tangled web of international conspirators suspected of being involved in the 1993 WTC bombing began to unravel with an initial investigation in the World Trade Center's own backyard. Across the Hudson River in Jersey City, New Jersey, were the headquarters of Islamic fundamentalist Sheik Omar Abdel-Rahman. One of his many followers was a young Palestinian by the name of Mohammad Salameh. Government agents realized that Salameh was the key to the door of a clandestine terrorist cell (a cell is the smallest unit of an organization). Opening that door would shed light on other shadowy figures, including the writer of the letter mailed to *The New York Times* that claimed responsibility for the February 26 bomb.

Mohammad Salameh was only a low-level player in the cell's history. He was not the brains behind the operation. He never figured that his compulsion to reclaim a four hundred dollar deposit paid for the rental van made him an instant target of suspicion by the FBI. Lawyers later pointed to this incident as evidence of Salameh's innocence. Why would a guilty man openly attract such unwanted attention to himself? Government agents claimed Salameh was not smart enough to realize what he was doing.

Whatever the case, FBI agents arranged a trap and lured Mohammad Salameh into it by promising the Palestinian that his deposit would be refunded if he returned in person to the rental agency to collect it. Salameh agreed. The trap was set.

The news of the connection between the rental agency in New Jersey and the van used to transport the bomb was somehow leaked to major television networks. The original plan of the FBI was to refund Mohammad Salameh's deposit and then to keep him under surveillance. It was hoped that Salameh would lead the FBI to other suspected terrorists. Unfortunately, the plan backfired.

News trucks and camera crews arrived at the site of the trap in order to broadcast the breaking news story. It was quickly decided that under the circumstances, keeping Salameh under surveillance was too risky. Instead, Mohammad Salameh was arrested on the spot. He was taken into custody on March 4, 1993—less than a week after the bombing.

After the arrest of Mohammad Salameh, a search of his personal property led to a number of other suspects. The first was Nidal Ayyad, a chemist who worked for the Allied Signal Corporation in New Jersey. Federal agents quickly connected Ayyad to Salameh through telephone toll records and bank accounts the two men shared.

In some ways, Nidal Ayyad puzzled agents investigating the bombing. Ayyad did not fit the mold of a typical terrorist. He seemed more of a typical American success story. Nidal Ayyad had been born in Kuwait. He was in his mid-twenties and was a naturalized American citizen—that is, he had sworn loyalty to the United States and been granted legal citizenship, with all of the rights and duties of an American citizen. He lived with his divorced mother and two younger brothers in New Jersey. His father lived in Jordan. Nidal Ayyad had attended Rutgers, a state university in New Jersey, and earned a degree in chemical engineering.

Mohammad Salameh and Nidal Ayyad were not only associates, but close friends. Salameh carried a photograph of himself and Ayyad in his wallet. In the photo, Mohammad Salameh and Nidal Ayyad were posed with another man near New York's Empire State Building. The other man was identified as El Sayyid Nosair.

Agents discovered that large sums of money had been deposited and withdrawn from Salameh's and Ayyad's joint accounts on a regular basis. The source of the money could not be determined, but much of the money was spent to fund the needs of an organization to which Mohammad Salameh, El Sayyid Nosair, and Nidal Ayyad belonged. That organization was the Liberation Army, involved in the bombing of the World Trade Center.

When agents raided the living quarters and office of Nidal Ayyad, they seized his personal computer. A search of the personal files in Ayyad's computer revealed wording identical to the text of the letter sent to *The New York Times* claiming responsibility for the bombing.

A Bomb Factory

Toll records and receipts discovered in Nidal's possession led investigators to a rented "safe house" used as a bomb factory to manufacture explosives. The bomb factory was located in a garage converted into two apartments in Jersey City, New Jersey.

When FBI and ATF agents raided the apartment, they found traces of nitroglycerin and urea nitrate (ingredients used in making explosives) on the carpet and the ceiling. It appeared that a chemical reaction involving acid had occurred at the site. They also learned that Mohammad Salameh had rented the apartment using an alias (a fake name). Evidence was starting to pile up against Salameh.

Additional phone records revealed that Mohammad Salameh and Nidal Ayyad had made frequent calls to a self-storage center not far from the Jersey City bomb factory.

A search of that storage area turned up items used in bomb making. Among items seized by government agents were 300 pounds of urea, 250 pounds of sulfuric acid, containers for nitric acid and sodium cyanide (some full and some empty), long lengths of fuse, a pump, and a white crystalline substance identified as urea nitrite. Everything needed to make a bomb was stored at the site. Agents interviewed the manager of the center and learned that Mohammad Salameh had rented the space under the name of Abraham Kamal. The manager also told the investigators several "Arab-looking" men were seen using a Ryder van at the center days before the bombing.[2] He then detailed an incident that had occurred February 25, 1993, the day before the WTC attack.

Salameh (known to the manager as Kamal) was at the site with another man (later identified by the agents as Ramzi Yousef). Salameh and Yousef were there to receive a delivery of three large cylinders of compressed hydrogen gas. The assistant manager of the storage center refused to let Salameh store the containers at the site. It was too dangerous. The gas could explode under certain conditions. After a heated discussion, Salameh was allowed to let the containers rest outside of the storage area until friends in a van and a car arrived to transport them elsewhere.

The Ringleader

Ramzi Yousef illegally entered the United States in September of 1992 using a phony Iraqi passport. Yousef was a native of Pakistan whose real name was Abdul Basit Karim. Ramzi Yousef was known by Interpol (the international police agency) as a Muslim radical and terrorist. Yousef's family lived in Quetta, a frontier city of Pakistan near a remote border with Afghanistan. Ramzi

Yousef had his training as a terrorist in Afghanistan. Police in Israel had files that connected him to the terrorist groups Hamas and Fatah. Yousef was well trained in the art of building and planting explosives. He regularly used a dozen or more aliases to hide his true identity. When he entered the United States at Kennedy International Airport in 1992, he presented a valid passport. However, he did not have a visa. (A visa is an endorsement made on a passport allowing the bearer to enter a particular country.)

"I want political asylum," Yousef told the agents from the Immigration and Naturalization Service (INS) who interviewed him.[3] Yousef was requesting that he be granted refuge in the United States. At first, the agents were suspicious. Then Yousef spun an intriguing tale of being persecuted by brutal Iraqi soldiers because he was a member of a Kuwaiti guerrilla organization. Yousef begged the agents not to return him to Iraq. His phony story was accepted, and terrorist Ramzi Yousef was allowed to enter the United States.

Ramzi Yousef adopted the name of Rashiid for his stay in the United States. He quickly hooked up with one of his key contacts—Mahmoud Abouhalima. With the help of Abouhalima, Yousef managed to get a New York City cab driver's license. He then became Salameh's roommate.

Using the alias of Abraham Kamal (the same name Salameh used to rent the self-storage space in Jersey City), Yousef went to a chemical company and purchased the chemicals necessary to construct a massive bomb. The chemicals were delivered to the storage site and transported to the bomb factory as needed.

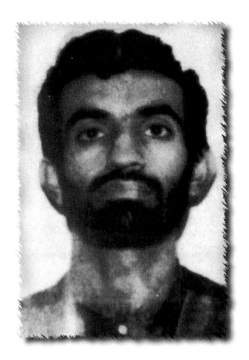

Ramzi Yousef was believed to be the leader of the bombing ring. In 1992, he entered the United States illegally by claiming to be a Kuwaiti refugee.

Mahmoud Abouhalima, an Egyptian, worked in Edison, New Jersey, at a filling station. Mahmoud was often called "The Red" by fellow Muslims because the big man had red hair and freckles. In Middle Eastern folklore, people with red hair and freckles are said to have "crusader blood." (The crusaders were Western Europeans who invaded what was then called Palestine during the eleventh to the thirteenth centuries in order to gain control of Christian holy places from the Muslims.) Abouhalima believed himself to be on a holy mission to destroy Western culture. As a young man, he supported Sheik Omar Abdel-Rahman's call to overthrow Egypt's secular leaders and to restore Egypt to a spiritual center of Arab culture.

Abouhalima left Egypt just days before President Sadat was assassinated. Abouhalima was wanted by Egyptian authorities for questioning about the murder, but he fled to Germany, where he asked for and received asylum. During the trial of Sheik Omar Abdel-Rahman for Sadat's murder, Abouhalima remained in Germany. He lived there until the mid-1980s. He then entered the United States illegally.

In 1986 Abouhalima was working as a taxi driver in New York City. It was at that time that he cultivated a friendship with fellow Egyptian El Sayyid Nosair.

Mahmoud Abouhalima then secured a permit to work in the United States as a noncitizen (sometimes called a "green card" because it is mostly used by foreign farmworkers). He claimed to be a farmworker, which was untrue. The green card allowed him to stay in the United States legally.

In the 1980s, the people of Afghanistan were involved in a bitter conflict with invading troops from the Soviet Union. (The United States opposed the Soviet invasion but did not send troops.) Muslim scholars, including Sheik Omar Abdel-Rahman, declared resistance to the Soviet invasion a "jihad." A jihad is a holy war waged by Muslim warriors to protect their religion. The struggle in Afghanistan became not only a political but also a religious conflict. Abdel-Rahman sent two of his sons to fight with the Afghan rebel forces. The sheik himself was a frequent visitor to Afghani rebel camps (his blindness prevented him from taking an active role in combat).

Inspired by the sheik's words and actions, Mahmoud Abouhalima left the United States and went to Afghanistan to fight the Soviets. He fought with elite Afghani guerrillas called the "Mujahedeen" for nearly two years.

Abouhalima returned to the United States in 1989 and became involved in the Alkifah Afghan Refugee Center in Brooklyn, New York. It was the Alkifah Afghan group that helped bring Sheik Omar Abdel-Rahman into the United

States. When Abdel-Rahman arrived in America, Mahmoud Abouhalima became his trusted chauffeur and bodyguard.

The Rest of the Terrorist Group

Ahmad Ajaj attempted to enter the United States illegally from Pakistan in September 1992 along with Ramzi Yousef. When questioned by INS agents at the airport, he produced a passport that identified himself as Khurram Khan. The passport aroused the suspicion of the agents. Ajaj looked Middle Eastern, yet his passport was Swedish. He offered a weak explanation.

"My mother was Swedish," Ajaj announced loudly. "My father was Pakistani."[4]

Ajaj seemed overly nervous and impatient. His behavior attracted the attention of other agents. His passport was examined more closely. It was discovered that Ajaj had pasted a photograph of his own face over the real passport photo. Ahmad Mohammed Ajaj was quickly arrested.

When Ajaj's luggage was examined, agents made a startling discovery. In the luggage were manuals and video-tapes describing different methods of manufacturing explosives. The explosives described were the types later used in the WTC bombing. Ajaj was held for questioning.

Other people were later linked to the conspirators. The names of two of the key terrorists were Eyad Ismoil and Abdul Rahman Yasin.

Eyad Ismoil was linked to the conspirators by phone records. Ismoil, a Jordanian, was a longtime associate of Ramzi Yousef. The two men had been high school friends in

Kuwait. Ismoil had studied at the University of Kansas. His relatives in Jordan told the press that he loved Western movies, hamburgers, and everything American.[5]

Ismoil lived in Dallas, Texas, but flew to New York City five days before the February 26 bombing. Government investigators believe that Eyad Ismoil drove the rental van containing the bomb into the parking basement of the World Trade Center. He was also accused of assisting Ramzi Yousef in setting the fuse of the bomb.

Abdul Rahman Yasin, an American citizen, was an associate and co-conspirator of Mahmoud Abouhalima, Nidal Ayyad, and Mohammad Salameh. Yasin lived at various places in New York and New Jersey. He assisted in transporting chemicals to and from the storage area and also helped construct the bomb at the bomb factory. Yasin was involved in transporting the bomb to the WTC site.

A Destructive Scenario

The World Trade Center bombing puzzle was pieced together after six months of intensive investigation. The story went something like this:

- Mohammad Salameh, Nidal Ayyad, Ramzi Yousef, Mahmoud Abouhalima, Eyad Ismoil, and Abdul Rahman Yasin were members of or connected with the Liberation Army, an Islamic terrorist group.

- Working together, Salameh, Ayyad, Abouhalima, and Yasin rented sites in New Jersey to store chemicals for making a bomb.

- Ramzi Yousef, a well-traveled world terrorist, entered the United States illegally to supervise the construction of the homemade bomb.

- Ahmad Ajaj was supposed to help build the bomb, but he was arrested at the airport when manuals on bomb-making were found in his suitcases.

- The members of the terrorist cell constructed the explosive device at a "bomb factory" in New Jersey.

- Eyad Ismoil, an old associate of Yousef who was already living in the United States, traveled from Texas to New York to help Ramzi Yousef transport and activate the bomb.

- Abdul Rahman Yasin helped in driving his fellow terrorists to and from the World Trade Center.

- On February 26, 1993, a bomb exploded in the basement parking area of the World Trade Center at eighteen minutes past noon on an ordinary workday. Six innocent people were killed by the blast. Over one thousand more were injured.

- After the attack, Salameh, Ayyad, and Ajaj remained in the United States. Ahmad Ajaj had no choice in the matter; he was already in jail. Yousef, Ismoil, Yasin, and Abouhalima all quickly fled the country and became the targets of an intense worldwide manhunt.

That manhunt would lead to the arrest of many other suspected terrorists before they could carry out their plans. Others remained free to carry on their reign of terror.

chapter five

TERROR ON TRIAL

IN CUSTODY—"I'll talk!" shouted a panicky Nidal Ayyad as he was led away in handcuffs from his New Jersey home by agents of the Federal Bureau of Investigation.[1] Ayyad later regained his composure and fell silent. He never did tell investigators what he knew about the 1993 WTC bombing.

Strangely enough, it was another member of the group who would later offer to give prosecutors valuable information about the 1993 WTC explosion. That was the battle-tested Afghani freedom fighter Mahmoud Abouhalima.

Abouhalima, the New York City taxi driver known as "The Red," fled to Egypt the day after the 1993 WTC bombing. He was identified in the United States through photos and eyewitness accounts. He was arrested in Egypt and extradited to the United States. (Extradition is the surrender of an accused person by one nation or jurisdiction to another.) Abouhalima would stand trial with Nidal Ayyad,

Ahmad Ajaj, and Mohammad Salameh, who were already in custody.

At first, Abouhalima was interrogated by Louis Napoli, a detective with the anti-terrorist task force handling the investigation. Through a careless slip of the tongue, Abouhalima associated himself with a man known as Rashiid, who was really Ramzi Yousef. It was the first, but not the last, of Abouhalima's loose-lipped chats.

The Legal Defense

In the United States, a person is presumed innocent until proven guilty in a court of law. The U.S. justice system follows strict legal procedures to ensure the rights of anyone charged with a crime, no matter how terrible that crime may be. Every defendant is entitled to be represented by legal counsel. Defendants have to feel sure that their lawyers are doing the best job possible to present their side of the case.

Mahmoud Abouhalima realized he needed a good lawyer. He contacted a famous defender named William Kunstler. Kunstler had worked for many controversial clients in the past. Even though he was Jewish, Kunstler had defended El Sayyid Nosair in the Meir Kahane murder case and won an acquittal. He had also worked as defense attorney for the celebrated Chicago Seven, political protesters who were tried for conspiracy to riot at the 1968 Democratic National Convention. Kunstler had won an acquittal in 1987 for Bronx drug dealer Larry Davis, who was accused of shooting several New York city policemen. He is probably best known for defending Jack Ruby, who

El Sayyid Nosair, another member of the Liberation Army, was implicated in the murder of Rabbi Meir Kahane, a Jewish militant.

shot and killed Lee Harvey Oswald, the man who assassinated President John F. Kennedy.

Abouhalima pleaded with Kunstler for help. Kunstler refused to handle the case himself. However, the well-known defense lawyer did offer the names of attorneys who might be able to help Abouhalima and his friends.

At Kunstler's suggestion, Mahmoud Abouhalima hired Jesse Berman, a skilled defender in high-profile, politically sensitive cases. In 1986 Berman defended the Ohio Seven, who were white revolutionaries charged with the 1983 bombing of military installations and government offices. Even though public opinion ran high against his clients at the time, Berman managed to punch holes in the prosecution's case. His clients were eventually acquitted.

Also at the urging of William Kunstler, Nidal Ayyad hired Leonard Weinglass to present his defense. Weinglass was one of William Kunstler's old partners. The two attorneys had worked together on the Chicago Seven case. Weinglass knew the ropes when it came to defending an unpopular client in a highly publicized case.

Ahmad Ajaj selected Lynne Stewart, a top female

defense lawyer, to handle his case. She had teamed with William Kunstler on the Larry Davis case in 1986.

Robert Precht was a lawyer appointed by the court to defend Mohammad Salameh. Precht was capable, but not as famous or as experienced as the other defenders. At the time, his best claim to fame was that he was the grandson of famous television host Ed Sullivan.

Precht and Salameh did not always agree on the plan of defense, even though Precht enlisted the aid of his boss, John Byrnes, on the case. Despite Precht's efforts to inform him, Mohammad Salameh did not seem to grasp the seriousness of the charges against him. While in court during the pretrial stages, Salameh instructed his attorney to give a strange message to the news artists sketching him.

"Draw me like I am a human being, not a terrorist," Salameh said.[2]

The Prosecutors

The prosecution team was headed by Henry DePippo and J. Gilmore Childers, two young U.S. attorneys. Childers had been the prosecutor in the Meir Kahane murder case. He was adept in interviewing people of Middle Eastern descent. Both men were also deputy chiefs of the Manhattan U.S. Attorney's Criminal Division. They were assisted by attorneys Michael Garcia and Lev Dassin.

The Judge

The judge chosen to preside over the case was Kevin Duffy, a twenty-one-year veteran of the bench. He had been the judge in the famous 1983 Brinks truck robbery case, in which six African-American defendants stole $1.6 million and killed three people, including a police officer. The defendants claimed they wanted to start a new black nation called New Afrika to be located in the southern United States. That case attracted a lot of publicity, so Duffy was not inexperienced when it came to dealing with explosive, high-profile cases. The trial of the 1993 WTC bombers would prove to be such a case.

Confusion Before the Trial

While Mahmoud Abouhalima sat in jail awaiting trial, he began to talk. At first he talked frequently and freely with fellow prisoner Theodore Williams, a killer involved in drug trafficking. His inclination to talk did not go unnoticed by government officials.

Meanwhile, Judge Duffy did not want lawyers for the defense chatting with the press about the case. He issued a gag order, which prevented the defense and the prosecution from releasing public statements to the media.

As the time for the start of the trial neared, elements of the case took some perplexing turns. Attorney Lynne Stewart and her client, Ahmad Ajaj, could not agree on a defense plan. Ajaj felt he could not be successfully represented by Stewart. She was replaced by Austin Campriello, a seasoned defense attorney.

Attorney Jesse Berman went before Judge Duffy and asked for a continuance because Mahmoud Abouhalima could not afford to pay his fees. Berman wanted Duffy to grant Abouhalima time to raise the money. Judge Duffy refused and told Berman he would not name Berman a court-appointed defender (like Robert Precht), which would entitle him to a fee of $75.00 an hour. (This is far less money than would be charged by an attorney who is privately hired.) Because of the money issue, Berman was forced to withdraw from the case. Leonard Weinglass, Nidal Ayyad's attorney, was caught in a similar predicament. He, too, was compelled to drop the case. Mahmoud Abouhalima and Nidal Ayyad were now without counsel. The court could have eventually appointed attorneys for the men, but the lawyers would have to be acceptable to the defendants.

The lack of legal representation did not silence Abouhalima's chattering in jail. He told fellow prisoner Theodore Williams that the goal of the bombing was to force the U.S. government to free El Sayyid Nosair from Attica Prison in New York. Williams, a seasoned criminal, urged Abouhalima to make a deal with the prosecutors. Abouhalima thought that was a good suggestion. He decided it would be in his best interest to arrange a deal. He would try to exchange information about the bombing for the guarantee of a lighter sentence.

Mahmoud Abouhalima met with prosecutors DePippo and J. Gilmore Childers about the possibility of becoming a cooperating government witness—one who gives information to prosecutors in exchange for the reduction (or even elimination) of the sentence. Abouhalima wanted not only the guarantee of a reduced sentence, but also a cash payment for his testimony.

After about a week of interviews, DePippo and Childers advised Judge Duffy that Abouhalima was willing to talk. Duffy realized Abouhalima was speaking to prosecutors without the benefit of a defense counsel. No attorney had been appointed to represent Abouhalima. It had been an oversight on the part of the prosecutors, who were eager to hear what Abouhalima had to say. Of course, Judge Duffy realized the legal problems this raised. He ordered the interviews terminated. They immediately ceased. If Abouhalima wanted to talk, he could continue to do so when a defense attorney was present to protect his legal rights.

Ahmad Ajaj had already replaced Lynne Stewart with attorney Austin Campriello. Now Mahmoud Abouhalima also got a new attorney, Hassen Ibn Abdellah. Abdellah was an ex–Bucknell University football player who had earned his law degree in 1983 from Seton Hall University in New Jersey. Abdellah was assisted in Ahmad Ajaj's defense by law associate and fellow Muslim Clarence Faines.

Nidal Ayyad's new attorney was Atiq Ahmed, a

Ahmad Ajaj was in jail at the time of the WTC bombing. He had been arrested at the airport when bomb-making manuals were discovered in his luggage.

Muslim born in India. Ahmed practiced law in Silver Springs, Maryland.

The defense now counted Austin Campriello, Hassen Ibn Abdellah, Clarence Faines, Atiq Ahmed, and Robert Precht (who remained Mohammad Salameh's lawyer) among its ranks. It was apparent that the defense attorneys would function as individuals rather than work together as a team. As far as the 1993 WTC bombing conspirators were concerned, it was every man for himself.

One of the first things Abouhalima's new lawyer did when he became part of the case was to end his client's discussions with prosecutors. Abdellah felt that Abouhalima was facing a life sentence and would not benefit from cutting a deal. After all, what would his client's sentence be reduced to? Maybe fifty years? That would not be much of an improvement. Making a deal to become a cooperating government witness was senseless.

Other Informers, Plots, and Terrorists

The prosecutors could not use the testimony of Mahmoud Abouhalima to help build their case against the terrorists. However, another individual involved in the terrorist organization the defendants belonged to came forward. He was an informant already working for the FBI. He had provided information prior to the February bombing that FBI agents had not acted upon. Later he would provide information that would prevent other planned attacks. He would also name other men involved in terrorist activities.

The informant was Emad Salem, a former lieutenant colonel in the Egyptian Army.

At the time of the 1993 WTC bombing, Salem was a close associate of Sheik Omar Abdel-Rahman, the well-known Islamic scholar. Emad Salem was also a paid secret informant of the FBI. Salem had heard vague rumors of a possible terrorist attack before the WTC bombing; however, details were sketchy. Emad Salem warned his FBI contacts that Muslim militants working with Abdel-Rahman were planning bombings and assassinations, but no action was taken on the tip. It is impossible to know whether the WTC bombing could have been prevented if agents had heeded Salem's warning.

After the February 1993 attack, Emad Salem was offered a large sum of money to help expose the terrorist web around Sheik Omar Abdel-Rahman. For his assistance in the matter, Emad Salem would be paid $1.5 million.

Salem secretly recorded all of his conversations and meetings with the blind cleric. It was an ongoing investigation that made some startling revelations. The numerous hours of recordings that he supplied to the FBI exposed a terrorist network around Abdel-Rahman led by a Sudanese man named Siddig Ibrahim Siddig Ali.

Months after the WTC bombing, Emad Salem alerted his FBI contacts that the bombing was just one link in a proposed chain of deadly explosions. New targets included the Holland and Lincoln tunnels and the George Washington Bridge (which connect New York and New Jersey) as well as the Statue of Liberty and the United Nations building in New York City.

The role Sheik Omar Abdel-Rahman played in this ongoing terrorist threat to the United States was hazy. He was not actively involved in the production of the bombs or in carrying out any of the plans. However, the sheik was specifically involved in the planning of the attacks. He did know about the attacks and did nothing to prevent them. He also urged the Muslim militants to select military targets rather than public ones. His part in suggesting targets was recorded on tape. There was little doubt that Sheik Omar Abdel-Rahman was involved with terrorists. However, in a court of law his actions might not be considered criminal. By legal definition he was not a co-conspirator. Deciding exactly what crime the sheik was guilty of under U.S. law would require a great deal of thought at a later date.

This time the FBI acted on tips provided by Emad Salem. No chances were taken after the February 1993 attack. FBI agents raided a warehouse that was reputed to be a terrorist bomb factory in the Jamaica, Queens, section of New York. Twelve terrorists were caught red-handed manufacturing explosive devices.

"The subjects were actually mixing the witches' brew," New York FBI Director James Fox later told the press. "We entered so fast some of the subjects didn't know we were in the bomb factory until they were in handcuffs."[3]

After the raid on the warehouse in Queens, Abdel-Rahman sought refuge in the Abu Bakr Mosque in Brooklyn, New York. It was a stronghold of the sheik's followers. FBI officials did not want to arrest Rahman at that time. They had very little hard evidence against the religious leader and believed that if he remained at large he might draw other militants out of hiding.

However, there was political and public pressure to arrest Sheik Omar Abdel-Rahman. He was a well-known Islamic militant suspected of terrorist activities prior to coming to the United States. He was an outspoken supporter of terrorism. New York City comptroller Elizabeth Holtzman wrote to the justice department and demanded that he be taken into custody. New York Republican senator Alfonse D'Amato argued vehemently for his arrest. Even Egyptian authorities were urging U.S. officials to arrest Abdel-Rahman.

In July 1993, U.S. Attorney General Janet Reno announced that investigators would pursue a case of seditious conspiracy against Sheik Omar Abdel-Rahman. (Sedition is defined as inciting people to resist or rebel against established authority.) Prosecutors would charge Rahman with advocating the overthrow of the government of the United States. Sheik Omar was finally arrested. The arrest took place a little more than two months before the initial World Trade Center bombing trial was to begin.

The Case Against the Terrorists

The WTC bombing trial began in September 1993. It would not end until March 1994. It was a long, complex, and sometimes puzzling trial. In some instances it raised more questions than it answered.

Facing justice were four Muslim militants accused of terrorist conspiracy: Mohammad Salameh, Ahmad Ajaj, Nidal Ayyad, and Mahmoud Abouhalima. Ramzi Yousef, Eyad Ismoil, and Abdul Yasin were still fugitives at large.

It took eight days to select a jury to sit in judgment of the four accused terrorists. Numerous potential jurors were excused from participating for one reason or another. It was difficult to find twelve people in New York's southern district (which covered Manhattan, the Bronx, and Queens) who were not in some way affected by the February 26 explosion and could be impartial in rendering a just verdict.

Finally, a jury agreeable to both the prosecution and the defense was assembled. The forewoman was a young, college-educated African American from Westchester, New York.

There were some interesting aspects to the makeup of the jury. None of the jurors were Muslim. All were either Catholic or Protestant. Seven of the twelve were college graduates. Another three had high school diplomas. It was a well-educated

The Islamic fundamentalist leader Sheik Omar Abdel-Rahman lived in New Jersey. He was an influential teacher and supporter of terrorism. He was arrested in 1993 and charged with sedition.

jury that would have many complex facts to consider and examine.

The cases against Mohammad Salameh and Nidal Ayyad were strong. Witnesses identified Salameh as having been at the storage center where the men had kept explosive materials and at the bomb factory. Salameh had rented the van used to transport the bomb to the World Trade Center. His association with Ramzi Yousef was also established without question. It became clear that Salameh had led a double life. On the surface he appeared to be harmless, yet he was a secret terrorist.

Nidal Ayyad had also led a double life. He, too, appeared harmless. Yet the prosecutor displayed a photograph of him with a Palestinian flag over his shoulder and a live hand grenade clutched tightly in his fist. FBI agents had found the photo ripped up in his trash and pieced it together.

The evidence against Ayyad included the messages found in the private files of his personal computer. The most incriminating evidence against Ayyad came from a DNA test conducted by government agents. Ayyad's DNA matched DNA taken from saliva on the envelope holding the letter mailed to *The New York Times*, claiming responsibility for the bombing. There was no doubt that Nidal Ayyad had licked the flap of the envelope to seal it.

Nidal Ayyad had rented a car used for a scouting trip to examine the parking basement below the World Trade Center two weeks before the bombing. Witnesses also placed him at the bomb factory.

In addition, Salameh's and Ayyad's fingerprints were

found on materials used to make the bomb and in vehicles connected to the attack.

At first it appeared that connecting Ahmad Ajaj to the bombing would be difficult, since Ajaj was in jail at the time the explosion occurred. However, his role in the conspiracy soon became apparent. He had tried to enter the United States illegally at the same time as Ramzi Yousef, the ringleader of the plot. In his suitcase, Ajaj carried with him manuals and videos on bomb making. Yousef's fingerprints were found on those items.

While in jail, Ajaj had made numerous phone calls. Inmates are advised that phone conversations made from jail are not confidential. Officials could not only listen in on the calls, but could also record such conversations.

Ajaj had frequently called a friend in Dallas, Texas. Those calls had been patched through to Ramzi Yousef in New Jersey with the assistance of a three-way calling system. Ajaj's calls to Yousef confirmed that he was an active conspirator in the bombing scheme.

The case against Mahmoud Abouhalima was something less than airtight. He was connected to Salameh and Yousef, but just knowing someone is not a crime. A witness named Carl Butler identified Abouhalima and placed him at the bomb factory. Another witness, Willie Hernandez Moosh, a gas station attendant, was brought in to identify Abouhalima as one of a group of men who stopped at his station near the mouth of the Holland Tunnel to gas up a cab and a rented van in the early morning hours before the February 26 bombing. Unfortunately for the prosecution, Moosh became nervous on the witness stand and could not make a positive identification, much to the relief of Abouhalima.

Nevertheless, it was later established that Mahmoud Abouhalima had purchased black powder, a type of explosive. A pair of work shoes discovered at Abouhalima's residence also had sulfuric acid stains on them. Sulfuric acid was used at the bomb factory and further linked Abouhalima to the site.

A phone card belonging to Mahmoud Abouhalima was a key piece of evidence linking him to the conspiracy. The card traced calls to the other defendants, the chemical company, and the bomb factory.

The trial lasted for over six months. Some two hundred witnesses and over one thousand exhibits were introduced. There were ten thousand pages of testimony in all. It was a lot for the jury to digest.

No Case for the Defense

The attorneys for the defense were faced with overwhelming evidence against their clients. The defense attorneys did not have a joint plan to counter the prosecution's case. Their lack of unification limited their options. Each attorney pursued his own line of personal defense. No one seemed capable of coming up with a concrete way to dispute or challenge the evidence presented by the prosecution.

Reluctantly, Robert Precht, Salameh's attorney, decided not to present any defense at all. He refused to call witnesses to testify on the behalf of his client or to put his client on the witness stand. Atiq Ahmed, Ayyad's lawyer, also chose not to offer a defense. Ahmed would not attempt to refute the charges leveled against his client in court. Rather, Ahmed and Precht decided to let their clients take their chances with the case the prosecution presented against them. Defendants are presumed innocent. The prosecution would have to prove them guilty beyond a reasonable doubt. It was a risky choice. Hassen Ibn Abdellah, Abouhalima's attorney, felt that the testimony of Willie Hernandez Moosh and his inability to identify his client was defense enough. Abdellah believed that because his client was not positively connected to the terrorists by someone who was supposed to be a star witness for the prosecution, the jury would have doubts about Abouhalima's participation in the bombing. Hassen Ibn Abdellah did not offer any further defense.

Only Austin Campriello, Ajaj's attorney, presented any type of defense. Campriello tried to show that just because his client had bomb-making manuals in his possession did not mean he was a terrorist. The attorney demonstrated that ordinary citizens could obtain such materials quite easily. He called to the stand a private investigator named William Natio. Natio testified that he had purchased bomb-making manuals and videos like the ones found in Ajaj's luggage through a magazine aimed at mercenary soldiers. Such magazines advertise abroad. Austin Campriello tried to weaken the prosecution's case against his client by decreasing the importance of the evidence found in Ajaj's luggage. It was an interesting tactic, but would it work in his client's favor?

There were several questions about the actions of one defendant that could not be satisfactorily addressed by the prosecutors. Mohammad Salameh had listed his own name when renting the van used to transport the bomb. If Salameh was a terrorist, why would he incriminate himself? Wouldn't a terrorist use a fake name instead to cover his tracks? Salameh also listed a phone number where he could be reached. That phone number belonged to a man named Josie Hadas who lived in Jersey City, New Jersey. Salameh contended that Hadas had hired him to transport some cargo. Radical Muslim supporters of Salameh's innocence claim that the man known as Josie Hadas was an operative of Mossad, the Israeli secret police organization.[4]

Furthermore, bomb-making instructions in English were reported to have been found in Hadas's apartment. Josie Hadas was said to have vanished after the bombing.[5]

Muslim defenders of Salameh claimed that Israeli terrorists actually carried out the bombing of the World Trade Center and tried to blame the attack on radical Muslims. Events that occurred years later on September 11, 2001—the attack and destruction of the World Trade Center by Muslim terrorists on a suicide mission—would seem to undermine this controversial theory, but in criminal cases all possibilities must be considered.

Those same defenders of the 1993 bombers pointed out that Salameh reported the van stolen and eventually tried to recover his deposit, which normally would not be the actions of a guilty man. These are issues for consideration. If Salameh was not involved and was being framed, it is possible that others, such as Ajaj, might also be victims of circumstance.

Of course, a simple explanation might be that Mohammad Salameh was just not bright enough to be a good terrorist.

PEOPLE WITH KEY ROLES

CONSPIRATORS IN THE 1993 BOMBING

Ramzi Yousef
Mohammad Salameh
Mahmoud Abouhalima
Nidal Ayyad
Ahmad Ajaj
Eyad Ismoil
Abdul Rahman Yasin

TRIED FOR SEDITION

Sheik Omar Abdel-Rahman

OTHER CONSPIRATORS

El Sayyid Nosair
Ibrahim El-Gabrowny
Siddig Ibrahim Siddig Ali
Clement Hampton-El
Victor Alvarez
Tarig Elhassan
Mohammed Saleh
Fadil Abdelgani
Amir Abdelgani
Fares Khallafalla
Osama bin Laden, leader
    of Al Qaeda

INFORMANTS

Emad Salem
Abdo Haggag
Siddig Ibrahim Siddig Ali
Ishtiaque Parker

DEFENSE LAWYERS

William Kunstler
Jesse Berman
Leonard Weinglass
Lynne Stewart
Robert Precht
John Byrnes
Austin Campriello
Hassen Ibn Abdellah
Clarence Faines
Atiq Ahmed
Frank Handelman

JUDGES

Kevin Duffy
Michael Mukasey

PROSECUTORS

Henry DePippo
J. Gilmore Childers
David Kelly
Mary Jo White

The Verdict

Mohammad Salameh, Nidal Ayyad, Mahmoud Abouhalima, and Ahmad Ajaj were found guilty of thirty-eight charges, including conspiracy to blow up the World Trade Center, explosive destruction of property, and interstate transportation of explosives.

"It is injustice!" yelled Mohammad Salameh as he leaped from his chair and waved his finger at the jury.[6]

Nidal Ayyad rose from his chair and exclaimed, "Allah!" which is the Arabic word for God. "Allah Akhbar!" shouted Salameh. The Arabic words translate into "God is great."[7]

On May 24, 1994, Mohammad Salameh, Nidal Ayyad, Ahmad Ajaj, and Mahmoud Abouhalima appeared before Judge Kevin Duffy to be sentenced. The defendants had all dismissed their attorneys and defended themselves at the sentencing (this later became a key issue). Among those who spoke at the sentencing was Ed Smith, the husband of Monica Rodriquez Smith, who died in the bombing. Part of Smith's comments are as follows:

> Your honor conducted a trial here that focused on a long, difficult and perhaps abstract body of evidence. Judge Duffy, we ask that you remember the crimes committed just a few blocks away from this courtroom were not abstractions. . . . The crime is not the sum of concrete destroyed, pipes smashed, or millions spent. We who have buried our dead without a chance to lay a comforting hand on their heads ask that you remember this bombing as an act of multiple murder.[8]

Judge Duffy considered Smith's words and the words

Vito Rodriguez, brother of bombing victim Monica Rodriquez Smith, places flowers at a memorial to the victims of the 1993 bombing. Smith's husband, as well as relatives of others killed in the explosion, asked Judge Duffy to remember the victims when he sentenced the four conspirators.

and letters of other relatives who had lost loved ones in the bombing. The sentencing process was long and at times tedious. Each of the defendants made a speech. Some were long and rambling. The statements seemed to have no connection to the case. The only defendant to make any reference to the actual crime in his speech was Ahmad Ajaj, who called the incident "horrible." All of the other defendants simply voiced complaints or made political statements about U.S. policy in the Middle East.

In the end, Judge Duffy sentenced Salameh, Ajaj, Ayyad, and Abouhalima to each serve 240 years in prison for their roles in the World Trade Center bombing. The disgruntled defendants were taken from the courtroom to the high-security U.S. penitentiary at Lewisburg, Pennsylvania, to serve their lengthy sentences. However, the convicted bombers' days in court were not yet over.

Another Trial

In 1994, Sheik Omar Abdel-Rahman was brought to court to stand trial on a charge of seditious conspiracy. The Sedition Law was first written in 1789 to deal with British loyalists deemed enemies of the United States. It was also used during and after the Civil War to bring to trial individuals engaged in acts meant to destroy the Union. The Sedition Law is a complex and broad law used in rare instances. Sedition is not easy to prove in a court of law, because seditious acts are difficult to define in legal terms.

Sheik Omar Abdel-Rahman was not the only high-ranking Muslim leader in New York to be indicted on conspiracy charges involving the planned bombing of New York landmarks. El Sayyid Nosair was also named in the indictment, as were eight other lower ranking Muslim militants. They included Ibraham El-Gabrowny (Nosair's cousin), Clement Hampton-El, Victor Alvarez, Tarig Elhassan, Mohammed Saleh, Fadil Abdelgani, Amir Abdelgani, and Fares Khallafalla.

The aim of the group known as the Liberation Army was to use terrorism to pressure the United States to reduce support for Middle Eastern countries opposed to Sheik Omar Abdel-Rahman's brand of Islam. They included

Israel, Iraq, and Egypt. In addition to targeting U.S. bridges, tunnels, and landmarks, they planned to bomb sections of New York City, FBI offices, and federal buildings.

Egyptian president Hosni Mubarak and former U.S. President Richard Nixon were also targeted by the terrorists to be killed or kidnapped.

The case against Sheik Omar Abdel-Rahman was built around information secretly gathered by informants within the sheik's own organization. The informants included Emad Salem, Abdo Haggag (a computer programmer and close confidant of the sheik) and Siddig Ibrahim Siddig Ali. Ali was a computer expert who was a key member in the plot to blow up additional New York landmarks. Once apprehended by authorities, he chose to cooperate.

Informant Abdo Haggag swore that Sheik Omar Abdel-Rahman had ordered the failed assassination of Egyptian president Hosni Mubarak. He also revealed that El Sayyid Nosair, Mahmoud Abouhalima, and Clement Hampton-El were leaders of a terrorist cell involved in the assassination of Rabbi Meir Kahane.

Siddig Ibrahim Siddig Ali, a mastermind in the follow-up bombing plots after the WTC explosion, turned informant to avoid prosecution and implicated Abdel-Rahman in the conspiracy.

Emad Salem, while secretly recording a conversation, tried to bait Sheik Omar Abdel-Rahman into admitting involvement in all of the bombing plots, but failed to do so. The tapes only proved that the sheik was indeed aware of the bombing plots.

Government officials had many tapes of Rahman providing advice (mainly religious or political) to the accused conspirators. There were also tapes of sermons in which he preached that all Muslims must be terrorists. Beyond that, no concrete evidence existed linking the sheik to the World Trade Center bombing or the shooting of Meir Kahane. It was no secret that Rahman wanted Egyptian president Mubarak dead, but wishing a person dead is not a punishable crime.

Defense attorney Lynne Stewart contended that the sheik was a spiritual leader being prosecuted for his words rather than his actual deeds. Many people, including non-Muslims, believed that the evidence against Sheik Omar Abdel-Rahman was weak at best. After all, he had taken no part in the planning or execution of the plans. However, he was aware of the actions and did approve of them.

Sheik Omar Abdel-Rahman was found guilty of seditious conspiracy to oppose the U.S. government by force and violence. The verdict was based almost totally on the testimony of FBI informants.

"This case is nothing but an extension of the American war against Islam," the sheik said.[9] He was sentenced to life imprisonment without parole.

Co-conspirator El Sayyid Nosair was sentenced to life in prison for his role in the bomb plot and for his involvement in the Meir Kahane murder. Earlier he had been acquitted of that murder, but this time he was charged with "assassination" as part of the conspiracy charges. Nosair was cleared of committing the murder of Meir Kahane. He could

Egyptian president Hosni Mubarak (on right) is shown in a meeting with Yassir Arafat, leader of the Palestine Liberation Organization. Terrorists planned unsuccessfully to kidnap or assassinate Mubarak because of his opposition to radical Islamic fundamentalism.

not be tried twice for the same crime. However, he was found guilty of conspiracy, or planning to commit the murder.

"Because of the bombing of the World Trade Center, the government made up this case," Nosair insisted.[10] He swore his innocence and challenged the honesty of the American judicial system.

However, among the papers of El Sayyid Nosair discovered by FBI agents were these words:

> We have to thoroughly demoralize the enemies of God . . . by means of destroying and blowing up the towers that constitute the pillars of their civilization such as . . . the high buildings of which they are so proud.[11]

Ibrahim El-Gabrowny was sentenced to fifty-seven years in jail for conspiracy and other charges. Clement Hampton-El, Tarig Elhassan, Victor Alvarez, and Mohammed Saleh each received sentences of thirty-five years in jail for their parts in the plot.

"I am not a terrorist!" Saleh cried at his sentencing. "I condemn terrorism in the world."[12] His words fell on deaf ears.

Other defendants involved in the conspiracy also received stiff sentences. The evidence against them had been more conclusive. They had actually been videotaped mixing chemicals for bombs. Fares Khallafalla received a sentence of thirty years. Amir Abdelgani was also sentenced to serve thirty years in prison. Fadil Abdelgani (Amir Abdelgani's cousin) was sentenced to a term of twenty-five years.

Perhaps the most chilling comment of all was uttered by a despondent Clement Hampton-El at the sentencing. He turned to the court and warned, "You'll be next. . . . The day will come for you."[13]

chapter six

A WORLDWIDE MANHUNT

IN PURSUIT—"There is no place where you are safe if you commit an act of terrorism against the United States."[1] Those words were spoken by John Coffee, a professor at Columbia University Law School in New York. His comments were directed at Ramzi Yousef, the man determined by the FBI to be the mastermind of the 1993 World Trade Center bombing.

A dedicated group of special agents was put together to gather evidence against fugitive Ramzi Yousef. Their jobs were to track him down, capture him, arrange extradition back to the United States, and, finally, secure a conviction against him in an American court of law. The joint terrorist task force team included FBI agents Neil Herman, Frank Pelligrino, and Charles Stern and Secret Service agent Brian Parr.

In addition, an agent from the FBI's elite counter-terrorist section, John Lipka, was directed to help chase down Ramzi Yousef. Lipka had studied Arabic and Farsi (a language spoken in Iran and Western Afghanistan) and had links to law officers in Pakistan. One of those links was to Rehman Malik, the director of Pakistan's Federal Investigation Agency, or FIA (Pakistan's equivalent of the American FBI).

The task force was assisted in the United States by agents from the New York Police Department, the Immigration and Naturalization Service, the State Department, and the Port Authority of New York and New Jersey. The agents realized that locating Ramzi Yousef and his co-conspirators, Eyad Ismoil and Abdul Rahman Yasin, would not be an easy task. It would require the complete cooperation of all the agencies involved, diligence, and a little luck.

After the 1993 bombing of the World Trade Center, Ramzi Yousef boarded a commercial aircraft and flew out of the United States. He used a passport that bore his real name, Abdul Basit Karim. Yousef flew to Karachi (Pakistan's largest city) and then quickly boarded a connecting flight to the remote city of Quetta. Yousef's wife and child lived in Quetta, as did his two younger brothers.

Quetta is a frontier city populated mostly by nomadic traders. It is just across the border from the Afghan city of Kandahar. It is a secluded place where strangers and foreigners are not usually welcome.

Yousef was relatively safe in the remote area. In fact, months passed before his presence in Quetta was discovered by his pursuers. When a team made up of agents from

Pakistan's FIA and the U.S. Diplomatic Security Service finally raided the house in Quetta where Ramzi Yousef was reportedly staying, Yousef was already long gone.

A chilling side note to the manhunt for Ramzi Yousef concerned Saudi millionaire terrorist Osama bin Laden. At the time evidence was uncovered that established close ties between bin Laden and Yousef's uncle Zahid Al-Shaikh. The two men were not only associates, but friends. Al-Shaikh was a senior figure in Mercy International, a Saudi-funded charity providing assistance to Afghan veterans and refugees. Osama bin Laden was closely affiliated with that organization.[2]

While in Pakistan, Ramzi Yousef did not keep a low profile to dodge the large group of agents dogging his trail. With several other radical militants, he quickly became involved in a plot to assassinate Benazir Bhutto, the former prime minister of Pakistan who was again running for the office. When a botched bombing attempt on her life in July 1993 resulted in injuries to Ramzi Yousef's eyes and face, he checked into a hospital in Karachi. He remained in the hospital under the name of Adam Baluch for several days. Apparently, Yousef felt perfectly safe and did not believe he was within the reach of U.S. law enforcement.

A Reward and Captures

To aid in the search for Ramzi Yousef, the United States government posted a hefty reward. The sum of $2 million was offered to anyone who would help bring the elusive Ramzi Yousef to justice. It was hoped that an informant would eventually turn Yousef in. Photographs and descriptions of the wanted man were widely circulated throughout the Middle East. U.S. agents hoped the reward and publicity would help tighten the noose around Yousef's neck and curtail his brazen acts of terrorism.

"The Yousef fugitive investigation was being very strongly pursued from the beginning, however it intensified again at the beginning of 1994, and we made an even bigger push," said Special Agent Neil Herman.[3]

Ramzi Yousef was tracked from Pakistan to Thailand. There he met with members of an Islamic militant group and became involved in a plot to bomb the Israeli Embassy. When the plot fizzled, Yousef returned to Pakistan. It is believed that he was then involved in a bombing in Iran designed to inflame grievances between Shiite and Sunni Muslims.

Ramzi Yousef once again left Pakistan and traveled to the Philippines. While living in the Philippines, Yousef worked on developing tiny but powerful liquid bombs. He was also linked to a plot (hatched by Osama bin Laden) to assassinate then U.S. President Bill Clinton. President Clinton was scheduled to visit the Philippines in 1994 at the start of a five-day tour of Asia. The plan to kill the president was eventually scrapped because security around Clinton was deemed too tight.

In December 1994, Ramzi Yousef was involved in a terrorist plot that led to his undoing. The tiny bombs that Yousef had worked on in the Philippines were finally put to use. Yousef concealed explosive components in his shoes and boarded an airliner at Manila Airport. He used an Italian

Osama bin Laden is head of Al Qaeda, an international terrorist organization whose name translates as "the base." He is believed to have planned the attack that toppled the World Trade Center in 2001.

passport that identified him as Armaldo Foriani. While in flight, he quietly assembled the tiny bomb and concealed it under a seat. When the plane reached Mactan Airport in the city of Cebu, Philippines, Ramzi Yousef disembarked from the aircraft. The plane then took off and continued toward its final destination of Tokyo, Japan. Hours later, the tiny bomb exploded. The blast blew a hole in the plane's floor and severed cables that controlled the plane's flaps. A young Japanese engineer named Haruki Ikegami was horribly maimed by the explosion and later died. Others were injured. Miraculously, the pilot managed to land the plane safely. Ramzi Yousef had struck again, but his reign of terror was finally coming to an end.

Yousef was tracked to a Manila apartment by officers of the Filipino National Police. When they arrived, Yousef was already gone, leaving behind evidence of his bomb-making activities.

Ramzi Yousef again returned to Pakistan. One of his associates and co-conspirators was a man named Ishtiaque Parker. Parker grew fearful of his risky relationship with Yousef and was tempted by the $2 million reward. Ishtiaque

Parker was supposed to help Yousef plant more bombs in planes from Asian countries destined for the United States. Instead, Ishtiaque Parker phoned FIA officials in Islamabad, Pakistan.

In February 1995, Parker told Pakistani officials that he knew the whereabouts of one of the world's most wanted men, Ramzi Yousef. Eventually Ishtiaque Parker was interviewed by Rehman Malik of the FIA.

The FIA quickly and quietly made arrangements with the FBI to arrest Yousef based on information provided by Ishtiaque Parker. In 1995, the manhunt for Ramzi Yousef finally ended. Agents of the FIA and the FBI, led by Ishtiaque Parker, crashed through the door of an apartment in Islamabad and arrested Yousef.

Ramzi Yousef was extradited to the United States to stand trial for the 1993 World Trade Center bombings. Money proved to be the bait that helped snare one of the world's most brazen and elusive terrorists. The cost was $2 million.

In 1995 Eyad Ismoil, the driver of the van that carried the bomb into the parking basement of the World Trade Center, was apprehended. Ismoil had been the target of an intense international manhunt. He was arrested in Jordan in August 1995.

The capture of Ismoil was applauded by President Bill Clinton. "Once again, we have shown that terrorism will not pay," Clinton told reporters.[4]

FBI agents tracked Ismoil to his parents' home in Jordan

and brought him back to the United States only six months after nabbing Ramzi Yousef in Islamabad.

With Ramzi Yousef and Eyad Ismoil in U.S. custody, only one terrorist, Abdul Rahman Yasin, remained at large.

Yousef in Court

In May 1996, Yousef appeared in U.S. Federal Court to face charges of conspiring to plant bombs on American airplanes. Yousef chose to handle his own defense in the case against the advice of Judge Kevin Duffy. In a calm statement to the jury, Ramzi Yousef stated:

> I want you to keep in mind that even though defendant Yousef [as he referred to himself] is not a U.S. citizen, and doesn't speak the way you speak, that he is a person just like you. Concentrate on the evidence. If you do so, the only just verdict is not guilty.[5]

Apparently, Yousef did not see the evidence the same way the jury did. Ramzi Yousef was convicted of killing Haruki Ikegami with the bomb he smuggled aboard the flight from Manila to Tokyo. He was also convicted of plotting a conspiracy to plant liquid bombs on a dozen U.S. airliners flying in from Asian cities in 1995. For his roles in the crimes, Ramzi Yousef was sentenced to life in prison. Next he would have to stand trial for the part he played in the 1993 bombing of New York's World Trade Center.

The Bombing Trial of Yousef and Ismoil

The trial for the 1993 bombing of the World Trade Center in New York City began amid a new terrorist scare. Just days before the start of the trial, a plot to blow up New York's subway system was discovered. New York City police officers, alerted by an informant, broke into what they believed to be a bomb factory and arrested three suspects with Middle Eastern backgrounds. One of the men arrested was Gazi Ibrahim Abu Mezer, a member of a known terrorist organization with links to the Islamic terrorist group Hamas.

Amid the threat of continued terrorist attacks, the trial of Ramzi Yousef and Eyad Ismoil began. This time Ramzi Yousef decided not to defend himself and was represented by counsel. The presiding judge was again Kevin Duffy. The lead prosecutor was David Kelly.

As in the previous trials, masses of evidence were presented. The government tried to show that Ramzi Yousef had entered the United States with the intent to cause injury. Prosecutor David Kelly claimed that Yousef arrived in the United States with one goal in mind: to bomb American targets. He further stated that both Ramzi Yousef and Eyad Ismoil felt they

Ramzi Yousef and Judge Kevin Duffy are shown in an artist's sketch made during Yousef's trial. Judge Duffy sentenced Yousef to life in prison for conspiring to blow up U.S. airliners.

had the right to "incinerate human beings for some twisted form of protest."[6]

Prosecutor Kelly showed the jury thick blue manuals containing formulas for constructing bombs used by the terrorists.

"[Yousef's] fingerprints were all over them," Kelly said. "Yousef bragged to [FBI] agents about what he did." The prosecutor stated, "Yousef's only regret was that [the bomb] didn't kill enough people. It didn't kill the quarter of a million people he was aiming for."[7]

In addition to the fingerprints on the explosion manuals, Yousef's fingerprints were found on the storage locker where some of the bomb-making elements were stored.

Much of the evidence presented had been gathered by technicians working in the FBI lab and used in the first WTC bombing case against Nidal Ayyad, Mahmoud Abouhalima, Mohammad Salameh, and Ahmad Ajaj. This evidence came into dispute.

Lawyers for the defendants questioned the validity of evidence gathered in the FBI labs. They argued that the reports may have been tailored to convict Ayyad, Abouhalima, and Salameh. However, Judge Duffy ruled that an FBI lab examiner would be allowed to testify that a twelve-hundred-pound urea nitrate bomb—the type of bomb constructed in the men's bomb factory—caused the World Trade Center blast. This evidence implicated Yousef.

Eyad Ismoil, who was shown to have used several aliases, claimed to be an innocent dupe. Ismoil said he believed the van he drove to the World Trade Center was filled with harmless containers of soap and shampoo. Prosecutor Kelly said that statement was "nothing more than a pathetic lie."[8] Kelly described Ismoil as a key participant in the conspiracy. Phone records showed that Ismoil telephoned Yousef frequently. Fingerprints showed he not only helped load the bomb Ramzi Yousef constructed into the rental van and drove it to the intended target, but he also helped set the timing fuse.

Finally, prosecutor David Kelly told the jury it had been shown indisputable scientific evidence that incriminated both Yousef and Ismoil. The prosecutor further described the defendants as "cowards who also left in their wake . . . an eternal pain."[9]

On Wednesday, November 12, 1997, Ramzi Yousef and Eyad Ismoil were found guilty on all charges of participating in the planning and execution of the 1993 World Trade Center bombing.

Sentencing

Judge Duffy sentenced Ramzi Yousef and Eyad Ismoil to each serve 240 years in prison. In addition, the judge suggested that only Yousef's attorneys be allowed to visit him in prison. Duffy did not want friends, reporters, or curiosity seekers to visit the terrorist. Since Yousef had more than forty aliases, Judge Duffy felt the defendant had abandoned his true family name and thus abandoned his family also. Therefore, visitation by any family member should be denied. The judge stated:

The restrictions I am imposing are undoubtedly harsh. They amount to solitary confinement for life. However the evil that Yousef espouses needs to be "quarantined." Your treatment will be no different than that accorded to a person with a virus which, if loosed, could cause plague and pestilence throughout the world.[10]

In addition, Judge Kevin Duffy also fined Ramzi Yousef the sum of $4.5 million.

Ramzi Yousef, the convicted terrorist, stood dumbfounded at the end of his day in court. Perhaps the words he had spoken just before the judge's sentencing had come back to haunt him.

Eyad Ismoil's mother, shown above with Ismoil's attorney, speaks with reporters during her son's trial. Along with Ramzi Yousef, Ismoil was found guilty of planning and carrying out the 1993 WTC bombing.

"Yes, I am a terrorist," boasted Ramzi Yousef publicly, "and I'm proud of it."[11]

The convictions of Ramzi Yousef and Eyad Ismoil did little to calm ordinary Americans who were now acutely aware of dangerous worldwide terrorist networks.

"What we see are a number of converging events that could signal a very likely possibility of an impending terrorist attack on American citizens or facilities either here or abroad," said Clark Staten, executive director of the Emergency Response and Research Institute, a private corporation that specializes in corporate security, terrorism, intelligence, military, and national security issues, after Yousef's and Ismoil's sentencing. "We would urge additional precaution and alertness on the part of all Americans . . . the distinct possibility even exists of an attack in the Continental United States."[12]

The truth of that somber warning would not become clear until years later on September 11, 2001, when terrorist suicide soldiers hijacked four American airliners and crashed them into targets in the United States—including the Twin Towers of the World Trade Center.

chapter seven

JUSTICE REVISITED

BACK TO COURT—The convictions of Ramzi Yousef and Eyad Ismoil seemed to bring limited closure to the 1993 World Trade Center bombing. Only U.S. citizen Abdul Rahman Yasin remained at large, the subject of a continuing manhunt. Yasin was believed to be hiding in Iraq or Iran.

Mohammad Salameh, Nidal Ayyad, Mahmoud Abouhalima, and Ahmad Ajaj filed appeals and returned to court in August 1998. However, in a 150-page ruling, the Second U.S. Circuit Court of Appeals denied their request for a retrial. A panel of judges had conducted a thorough review of the arguments raised by the four men and their defense team, which was headed by attorney Frank Handelman. The panel deliberated for several months before reaching a decision.

The appeals panel concluded that U.S. District Judge Kevin Duffy had indeed made a conscientious assessment of all the evidence to ensure that the men had received a fair trial.

The defense had argued that lab evidence had been gathered in a slipshod manner and then tailored to fit the aims of the FBI. The panel did not believe that was the case.

U.S. Attorney Mary Jo White, the lead prosecutor, was pleased by the ruling of the panel. White called the ruling "another step toward closure for the families of those who were killed and all the other victims of the bombing."[1]

Defense attorney Frank Handelman was disappointed by the decision. "They took seven months or so to make the decision, which gave us some hope," he said.[2]

Resentencing Ordered

The appeals panel refused to grant Salameh, Ayyad, Abouhalima, and Ajaj a new trial, but it did rule that the men should be resentenced by Judge Kevin Duffy. Irregularities at the original sentencing procedures were cited as the cause for the ruling.

At the sentencing, the convicted men had represented themselves and were without the benefit of legal counsel. The appeals court ruled that the men should not have been allowed to represent themselves at sentencing.

The manner in which the sentences were calculated was also an issue of concern to legal experts. Originally, Judge Duffy had calculated how many years each of the victims could have expected to live and sentenced each defendant to a year in prison for each year of life they deprived their

Supporters of Sheik Omar Abdel Rahman demonstrate during the trial of the sheik and his followers in 1996. Though there was no evidence that the sheik took part in planning to bomb the Twin Towers and other landmarks, he knew of the plots and did nothing to stop them.

victims of. Salameh, Ayyad, Abouhalima, and Ajaj had originally been sentenced to serve 240 years each in prison.

In October 1999, Mohammad Salameh and his three co-conspirators once again stood before U.S. District Court Judge Kevin Duffy.

Salameh was very vocal at the resentencing. He publicly stated that the United States should stop meddling in the Middle East and cease its support of Israel. Salameh warned that an act of God would eventually humble the United States and force it to crumble in the same way the Soviet Union had dissolved.

Mohammad Salameh also had high praise for dictator Saddam Hussein of Iraq, a recognized enemy of the United States. He claimed the United States was more of a dictatorship than Iraq was.

Judge Duffy finally responded to Salameh's long-winded ramblings. "If you had been convicted of this crime under those foreign governments, there would be no resentencing," Duffy said to Salameh. "You don't resentence a dead person."[3] Judge Duffy then ordered Mohammad Salameh to serve 116 years and 11 months in prison. He further ordered Salameh to pay a $250,000 fine and $250 million in restitution to his victims should this story ever be bought for book or movie rights.

The next to be resentenced was American citizen Nidal Ayyad, a graduate of Rutgers University in New Jersey. Ayyad bitterly stated that after the 1993 bombing, no Arab could hope for a fair trial in the United States. Judge Duffy disagreed. He claimed Ayyad had taken everything he could from his adopted country and then tried to kill its people with terrorism. He sentenced Nidal Ayyad to 117 years and one month in prison. He also received the same fine as Mohammad Salameh.

Mahmoud Abouhalima had nothing to say at his resentencing. He quietly stood by as Judge Duffy pronounced his sentence. Abouhalima was ordered to spend 108 years and four months in prison. His fine was the same as that of his co-conspirators.

The last defendant to face Judge Duffy for resentencing was Ahmad Ajaj. Ajaj's only comment was to repeat that he was innocent of all charges. The judge levied the same fine as before and ordered Ahmad Ajaj to serve 114 years and ten months in jail. The trials of the 1993 World Trade Center bombers were finally over.

Unfortunately, more terrorism was yet to come in America—with the Twin Towers of the World Trade Center as its main target.

chapter eight

THE TERRORISM CONTINUES

TERROR ATTACKS—The tragic events in New York City on September 11, 2001, stunned the civilized world. In the most devastating terrorist onslaught ever waged against the United States, nineteen knife-wielding hijackers took control of four jetliners. One plane crashed into the Pentagon in Washington, D.C. Another crashed in a Pennsylvania field after some passengers apparently banded together and overcame the hijackers. Two other planes slammed into the Twin Towers of the World Trade Center. The towers began to burn as jet fuel spilled from floor to floor. A short time later, the towers came crashing down. Thousands lost their lives in the suicide attack.

"Today, our nation saw evil," said President George W. Bush.[1]

The threat uttered by a member of the 1993 bombing conspiracy took on new meaning in light of the horrifying events of September 11, 2001. "Next time it will be very precise," terrorist Nidal Ayyad had written on his computer after the 1993 attempt to topple the World Trade Center towers.[2]

It was determined that the villains behind the attack were members of a worldwide terrorist network headed by Osama bin Laden. It was the same Osama bin Laden that Ramzi Yousef had connections to during his reign of terror.

"[The terrorists] have moved forward by enlisting more people willing to give up their lives for their idea of their religion," said Robert Blitzer, former Chief of Domestic Counter-Terrorism for the FBI in an interview in 2001. "They've constantly looked for bigger and better ways. This had been a logical progression."[3]

The comments of Blitzer made after the September 11 attacks were valid. In 1993, the terrorist bombing on the WTC occurred at the end of the month because the conspirators had run out of rent money. In 1993, the terrorists spent about four months planning the attack and used less than $100,000 to fund it.

In contrast, the September 11, 2001, attack on the WTC took several years to plan. Over $500,000 was spent to bankroll the attack. Terrorism is growing by leaps and bounds in terms of sophistication, cunning, and funding.

In the aftermath of the attacks of September 11, 2001, Osama bin Laden released a videotape made in Afghanistan, where he and his Al Qaeda network operated under the protection of the Taliban government. On the tape, an unidentified Arab sheik said to Osama bin Laden, "You have given us weapons, you have given us hope and we thank Allah for you . . . everybody praises what you did."[4]

The terrorists' prediction came true on September 11, 2001, when attacks leveled the Twin Towers of the World Trade Center. Shown are firemen working amid the wreckage.

Osama bin Laden's Al Qaeda terrorist network was not well known in 1993. It now seems obvious that Ramzi Yousef and some or all of his co-conspirators had some link to Al Qaeda.

In October 2001, President George W. Bush issued a "Most Wanted" list of twenty-two people wanted for their roles in terrorist crimes committed since 1985. On the list was Osama bin Laden, a citizen of Saudi Arabia, and Abdul Rahman Yasin, the U.S. citizen involved in the 1993 World Trade Center bombing.

"Now is the time to draw the line in the sand against the evil ones," President Bush said as he unveiled the list. "They must be found. They will be stopped, and they will be punished. This is the calling of the United States of America."[5]

The list includes the following people.

For the September 11, 2001, attacks on the World Trade Center and Pentagon and the bombings of U.S. Embassies in Kenya and Tanzania, August 7, 1998:

- Osama bin Laden—Saudi Arabia.

For the World Trade Center bombing, February 26, 1993:

- Abdul Rahman Yasin—U.S. citizen

For the plot to bomb Manila Aircraft in the Far East, January 1995:

- Khalid Shaikh Mohammed—Pakistan or Kuwait

For the Khobar Towers Building in Saudi Arabia, June 25, 1996:

- Ahmed IbrahimAl-Mughassil—Saudi Arabia
- Ali Said Bin Ali el-Houri—Saudi Arabia
- Ibrahim Salih Mohammed al-Yacoub—Saudi Arabia
- Abdeikarim Hussein Mohamed al-Nasser—Saudi Arabia

For the bombings of the U.S. embassies in Kenya and Tanzania, August 7, 1998:

- Muhammad Atef—Egypt
- Ayman Al-Zawahiri—Egypt
- Fazul Abdullah Mohammed—Comoros Islands
- Mustafa Mohamed Fadhil—Iraq
- Anas Al-Liby—Libya
- Abdullah Ahmed Abdullah—Egypt
- Sheikh Ahmed Salim Swedan—Kenya or Yemen
- Ahmed Khalfan Ghailani—Tanzania
- Fahid Mohammed Ally Msalam—Kenya
- Saif al-Adel—Egypt
- Ahmed Mohammed Hamed Ali—Egypt
- Muhsin Musa Matwalli Atwah—Egypt

For the hijacking of TWA flight 847, June 14, 1985:

- Imad Fayez Mugniyah—Lebanon
- Hassan Izz-Al-Din—Lebanon
- Ali Atwa—Lebanon

In the videotape released after the 2001 attacks on the World Trade Center, bin Laden said, "This event made people think, which benefited Islam greatly." The terrorist then made reference to the toppling of the Twin Towers and the massive loss of lives. "This is all that we had hoped for," he said.[6]

Concerned about the possibility of future terrorist attacks and the need to bring to justice those responsible for the September 11 attacks, President George W. Bush demanded that Afghanistan's Taliban government surrender Osama bin Laden in the fall of 2001. The president stated clearly that a refusal would likely result in military action against Afghanistan. After negotiations, peaceful means of dealing with the Taliban were exhausted.

Backed by support from all over the world, including vital assistance from Pakistan, Afghanistan's Northern Alliance troops, Uzbekistan, and other nearby countries, U.S. and British planes attacked Taliban and Al Qaeda strongholds in Afghanistan in October 2001. The attack proved to be the beginning of the end for the terrorist-friendly Taliban government. By the end of the year, the Taliban government had fallen. Yet many terrorists, including Osama bin Laden and Abdul Rahman Yasin, were still unaccounted for.

Terrorism Continues

Osama bin Laden and Abdul Rahman Yasin remained on the loose in 2003. The previous year had seen the arraignment of the first person to be prosecuted for the September 11, 2001, attacks: Zacarias Moussaoui, a French Muslim. Moussaoui, who was in jail on September 11, was charged with six counts of conspiracy because he was believed to have had prior knowledge of the attacks. He pleaded not guilty.

Just prior to the start of 2002, Richard Reid, an English Muslim, smuggled explosives concealed in his shoes aboard an aircraft bound for the United States. He apparently tried to follow in the footsteps of Ramzi Yousef but failed miserably. He was beaten down by fellow passengers when he tried to light the fuse attached to his shoe. Reid was subdued and turned over to authorities when the plane landed in the United States.

The war against terrorism worldwide is an ongoing conflict. It is a danger that can and will be faced by the United States, Great Britain, and other peace-loving nations.

"This nation is peaceful, but fierce when stirred to anger. This conflict . . . will end in a way and at an hour of our choosing," predicted President George W. Bush.[7]

Questions for Discussion

1. Do you believe the 1993 WTC bombing had any connection with the tragic events on September 11, 2001? If so, how?

2. Should the United States make it more difficult for foreigners to remain in America? Why or why not?

3. Do you think that the attorneys for Mohammad Salameh, Nidal Ayyad, Ahmad Ajaj, and Mahmoud Abouhalima should have presented no defense for their clients?

4. Was Sheik Omar Abdel-Rahman unjustly convicted? Why or why not?

5. Do you believe terrorists target sites in the United States because of America's relationship with Israel?

6. Do you think the prosecution of the people involved in the 1993 WTC bombing helped trigger the attack on the World Trade Center in 2001?

Chronology

1992—Members of militant Muslim groups have set up residences in the U.S. They include Sheik Omar Abdel-Rahman, Mahmoud Abouhalima, and Mohammad Salameh.

1992—Salameh, Abouhalima, Nidal Ayyad, and Abdul Rahman Yasin rent rooms and buy chemicals to start a bomb factory.

September 1992—Ramzi Yousef and Ahmad Ajaj arrive in the United States. Yousef enters the country using a fake passport. Ajaj is arrested.

February 1993—Militant Muslims construct a bomb. They transport it to the basement parking area of the World Trade Center in a rented van.

February 26, 1993—A bomb explodes below the World Trade Center, killing six people and injuring hundreds of others.

February 28, 1993—Detectives find and identify parts of the rental vehicle used to transport the bomb. The van is traced to Mohammad Salameh. Militant associates of Salameh are identified.

March 3, 1993—A letter from a militant group arrives at *The New York Times*. The group takes credit for the bombing.

March 4, 1993—Mohammad Salameh is arrested.

March 1993—Salameh is linked to Nidal Ayyad, El Sayyid Nosair, Sheik Omar Abdel-Rahman, and Mahmoud Abouhalima. Nidel Ayyad is found to be the writer of the letter to *The New York Times*, and he is arrested.

1993—Mahmoud Abouhalima is arrested in Egypt and returned to the United States. Agents connect Salameh, Ayyad and Abouhalima to Abdul Yasin, Ahmad Ajaj, and Ramzi Yousef.

September 1993—Trial of Mohammad Salameh, Nidal Ayyad, Mahmoud Abouhalima, and Ahmad Ajaj for the WTC bombing begins.

March 1994—Salameh, Ayyad, Abouhalima, and Ajaj are convicted.

1995—Ramzi Yousef is arrested in Pakistan and Eyad Ismoil is arrested in Jordan.

1996—Muslim militants Sheik Omar Abdel-Rahman, El Sayyid Nosair, and eight others stand trial and are convicted.

1997—Ramzi Yousef and Eyad Ismoil stand trial and are convicted.

October 13, 1999—Mohammad Salameh, Nidal Ayyad, Mahmoud Abouhalima, and Ahmad Ajaj are resentenced.

Chapter Notes

Chapter 1. Smoke, Terror, and Death

1. Larry Neumeister, "Terrorism More Sophisticated," *The* (Bridgewater, N.J.) *Courier-News*, October 1, 2001, p. A-10.

2. Ibid.

3. Mary Jo Patterson, "Tired Rescue Teams Seek Bodies Amid Collapsing Structures," *The* (Newark, N.J.) *Star-Ledger*, September 13, 2001, p. 1.

Chapter 2. A Plot Unravels

1. "Bomb Rocks New York," *The* (Bridgewater, N.J.) *Courier-News*, February 27, 1993, p. 1.

2. Ibid.

3. "Officials Confirm It Was Bomb," *The* (Bridgewater, N.J.) *Courier-News*, February 28, 1993, p. A2.

4. "Bomb Rocks New York."

5. "Officials Confirm It Was Bomb."

6. Jim Dwyer with David Kocieniewski, Deidre Murphy, and Peg Tyre, *Two Seconds Under the World: Terror Comes to America—The Conspiracy Behind the World Trade Center Bombing* (New York: Crown Publishers, 1994), p. 72.

7. "U.S. Has Never Had This Kind of Terror Blast," *The* (Bridgewater, N.J.) *Courier-News*, February 28, 1993, Special WTC Bombing Supplement.

8. Dwyer, Kocieniewski, Murphy, and Tyre, p. 74.

9. Ibid., p. 197.

Chapter 3. Islam and Terrorism: A History

1. Merle Severy, ed., *Great Religions of the World* (Washington, D.C.: National Geographic Society, 1978), pp. 223–226.

Chapter 4. Tracking the Terrorists

1. "World Trade Center Bombing Suspect Pleads Innocent," *The Detroit News/Reuters*, August 4, 1995, <http://www.detnews.com/menu/stories/12712.htm> (April 17, 2001).

2. David Williams, "The Bombing of the World Trade Center in New York City," *International Police Review*, No. 469–471, 1998, <Wysiwyg://55http://www.interpol.int/Public/Publications/ICPR/ICPR469_3.asp> (April 16, 2001).

3. Jim Dwyer with David Kocieniewski, Deidre Murphy, and Peg Tyre, *Two Seconds Under the World: Terror Comes to America—The Conspiracy Behind the World Trade Center Bombing* (New York: Crown Publishers, 1994), p. 163.

4. Ibid., pp. 162–163.

5. "World Trade Center Bombing Suspect Pleads Innocent."

Chapter 5. Terror on Trial

1. Jim Dwyer with David Kocieniewski, Deidre Murphy, and Peg Tyre, *Two Seconds Under the World: Terror Comes to America—The Conspiracy Behind the World Trade Center Bombing* (New York: Crown Publishers, 1994), p. 245.

2. Ibid., p. 249.

3. Simon Reeve, *The New Jackals—Ramzi Yousef, Osama bin Laden and the Future of Terrorism* (Boston: Northeastern University Press, 1999), p. 62.

4. "World Trade Center Bombing," *Institute of Islamic Information and Education*, n.d., <http://www.iiie.net/Articles/wtcbombing.html> (April 16, 2001).

5. Ibid.

6. Dwyer, Kocieniewski, Murphy, and Tyre, p. 291.

7. Ibid.

8. Ibid., p. 302.

9. "Sheik Gets Life Sentence in Terror Trial," *CNN Interactive*, January 17, 1996, <http://www.cnn.com/US/9601/terror_trial/update> (April 17, 2001).

10. Ibid.

11. George F. Will, "World of Terror," *New York Post*, September 14, 2001, p. 59.

12. "Sheik Gets Life Sentence in Terror Trial."

13. Ibid.

Chapter 6. A Worldwide Manhunt

1. Ron Scherer, "Bombing Trial Begins Amid Terrorism Scare," *The Christian Science Monitor*, August 4, 1997, <http://www.csmonitor.com/durable/1997/08/04/us.4.html> (April 17, 2001).

2. Simon Reeve, *The New Jackals—Ramzi Yousef, Osama bin Laden and the Future of Terrorism* (Boston: Northeastern University Press, 1999), p. 48.

3. Ibid., p. 63.

4. "World Trade Center Bombing Suspect Pleads Innocent," *The Detroit News/Reuters*, August 4, 1995, <http://www.detnews.com/menu/stories12712.htm> (April 17, 2001).

5. Reeve, p. 238.

6. Mary Ann McGann, "World Trade Center Suspect Called Bombing Ringleader," *CNN Interactive*, November 3, 1997, <http://www.cnn.com/US/9711/03/wtc.trial/> (April 17, 2001).

7. Ibid.

8. Ibid.

9. Ibid.

10. Reeve, p. 243.

11. Ibid., p. 242.

12. Paul Anderson, "Ramzi Yousef Found Guilty on Four Counts: ERRI Alert," *ERRI Daily Intelligence Report*, November 13, 1997, <http://www.emergency.com/alrt1197. htm> (April 17, 2001).

Chapter 7. Justice Revisited

1. "Court Upholds World Trade Center Bombing Convictions; Orders Resentencing," *CNN.com*, August 5, 1998, <http://www.cnn.com/US/9809/05/wtc.bombing.01> (April 17, 2001).

2. Ibid.

3. Larry Neumeister, "World Trade Center's Four Bombers Resentenced to Life Terms," *The Bergen Record*, October 14, 1999, p. A6.

Chapter 8. The Terrorism Continues

1. David Crary and Jerry Schwartz, "Terror Attacks Stun Nation," *The* (Bridgewater, N.J.) *Courier-News*, September 12, 2001, p. 1.

2. Larry Neumeister, "Terrorism More Sophisticated," *The* (Bridgewater, N.J.) *Courier-News*, October 1, 2001, p. 10.

3. Ibid.

4. Calvin Woodward, "Dinner with Osama bin Laden: All Eyes on the Special Guest," *The* (Bridgewater, N.J.) *Courier-News*, December 19, 2001, p. A-16.

5. David Espo, "Washington Continues Battle on Home Front After September 11 Attacks," *The* (Bridgewater, N.J.) *Courier-News*, October 11, 2001, p. A-13.

6. Woodward.

7. Larry McShane, "Bush Visits Devastation as Nation Unites in Grief," *The* (Bridgewater, N.J.) *Courier-News*, September 15, 2001, p. 1.

Glossary

Allah—Arabic for "God."

Al Qaeda—(Literally, "the base.") A worldwide terrorist network established by Osama bin Laden.

asylum—Refuge granted to a person or group fleeing from political, social, or religious persecution.

cell—The smallest unit of an organization.

conspiracy—A group of people acting together to carry out an illegal plan.

extradite—To return an accused person or fugitive from one nation or jurisdiction to another.

guerrilla—A member of an independent unit who carries out irregular warfare.

Hamas—A radical Islamic terrorist organization.

hijack—To take over a vehicle or craft by force.

Islam—The religion founded by the prophet Mohammad. The word means "submission to the will of Allah."

jihad—A holy war fought to protect followers of Islam and to preserve the faith.

militant—A person aggressively active in a particular cause.

Muslim—A follower of Islam. In Arabic, the word means "one who submits."

radical—A person who aims to make extreme changes in existing views, habits, or conditions.

sedition—Inciting people to resist or rebel against established authority.

sheik—An Arab tribal leader.

Taliban—A radical government that imposed an oppressive brand of Islam on the population of Afghanistan while supporting a terrorist network.

terrorism—Violence against noncombatants for political goals.

Further Reading

Books

Andryszewski, Tricia. *Terrorism in America*. Minneapolis, Minn.: Lerner Publishing, 1999.

Clark, Charles. *Islam*. Farmington Hills, Mich.: Gale Group, 2002.

Landau, Elaine. *Osama Bin Laden: A War Against the West*. Brookfield, Conn.: Millbrook Press, 2002.

Marcovitz, Hal. *Terrorism*. Broomall, Pa.: Chelsea House Publishers, 2001.

Shields, Charles J. *The World Trade Center Bombing*. Broomall, Pa.: Chelsea House Publishers, 2001.

Stewart, Gail. *America under Attack: September 11, 2001*. San Diego, Calif.: Lucent Books, 2002.

Streissguth, Thomas. *International Terrorists*. Minneapolis, Minn.: Oliver Press, 1999.

Internet Addresses

"The Bombing of the World Trade Center in New York City," International Criminal Police Review

<http://www.interpol.int/Public/Publications/ICPR/ICPR469_3.asp>

"The World Trade Center Bombing," Joint Terrorism Task Force ADL Law Enforcement Agency Resource Network

<http://www.adl.org/learn/jttf/wtcb_jttf.asp>

"World Trade Center History," Family Education Network

<http://www.factmonster.com/spot.wtc1.html>

Index